Runes
for Beginners

© Sarah O'Brien

About the Author

Dr. Alexandra Chauran (Issaquah, WA) is a second-generation fortune-teller, a high priestess of British Traditional Wicca, and the queen of a coven. As a professional psychic intuitive for over a decade, she serves psychic apprentices and thousands of clients. She received a master's in teaching from Seattle University and a doctorate from Valdosta State University and is certified in tarot. In her spare time, when she's not teaching students of Wicca, she enjoys ham radio with the call sign WI7CH. She can be found online at SeePsychic.com.

Runes

For Beginners

Simple Divination and Interpretation

Alexandra Chauran

Llewellyn Publications
Woodbury, Minnesota

First Edition
Seventh Printing, 2021

Cover art: iStockphoto.com/4875384/©Pshenichka
Cover design: Lisa Novak
Interior art: Llewellyn Art Department

Llewellyn Publications is a registered trademark of Llewellyn Worldwide Ltd.

Library of Congress Cataloging-in-Publication Data

Names: Chauran, Alexandra, author.
Title: Runes for beginners : simple divination and interpretation / by
    Alexandra Chauran.
Description: First Edition. | Woodbury : Llewellyn Worldwide, Ltd, 2016. |
    Includes bibliographical references.
Identifiers: LCCN 2016027039 (print) | LCCN 2016033430 (ebook) | ISBN
    9780738748283 | ISBN 9780738749785 ()
Subjects: LCSH: Runes—Miscellanea. | Divination.
Classification: LCC BF1779.R86 C43 2016 (print) | LCC BF1779.R86 (ebook) |
    DDC 133.3/3—dc23
LC record available at https://lccn.loc.gov/2016027039

Llewellyn Worldwide Ltd. does not participate in, endorse, or have any authority or responsibility concerning private business transactions between our authors and the public.

All mail addressed to the author is forwarded, but the publisher cannot, unless specifically instructed by the author, give out an address or phone number.

Any Internet references contained in this work are current at publication time, but the publisher cannot guarantee that a specific location will continue to be maintained. Please refer to the publisher's website for links to authors' websites and other sources.

Llewellyn Publications
A Division of Llewellyn Worldwide Ltd.
2143 Wooddale Drive
Woodbury, MN 55125-2989
www.llewellyn.com

Printed in the United States of America

Other Books by Alexandra Chauran

For Beginners

Featured In

I'd like to dedicate this book to my gods, the Lady of the Moon and the Lord of Death and Resurrection; to those who have trained me well in the Kingstone tradition of Wicca; and to the members of Lyra Star Coven who are always charmed by runes.

contents

introduction

Life is full of confusing decisions that might create big changes in one's life path months or years down the road. Sometimes it can feel like there's a fifty-fifty chance that what you're picking is the right choice for you. Perhaps you're trying to figure out whether or not to stay with a partner, wondering if he or she is the one for you. It could be that you're choosing between two college majors, each equally compelling and with similar job-market potential. These are huge decisions, and flipping a coin just doesn't seem to give these choices the respect they deserve. What if I told you that there's a way that you can connect to the divine and with your destiny that feels tangible? You can hold in your hands the key to your past, present, and future. Runes are sacred objects that you can touch and feel that allow you a sense of control over the mysteries of life. Runes are also concepts. Just as the word "love" written out on paper by your beloved can make your heart sing, runes were designed long ago to evoke feelings and a sense of wonder.

What Are Runes?

Runes typically refer to a collection of stones, pieces of wood, or other materials with sacred symbols inscribed upon them. Each rune tells a story. When runes are scattered on a surface, pulled from a bag, or carefully laid out in patterns, they can tell your life's story.

The word "rune" may come from the very old Proto-Germanic root word *run-,* meaning "secret," "whisper," or "mystery." The runes are forces of nature—mysteries in the religious sense of spiritual truths, rather than a mere puzzle to be solved. Essentially, runes are ideas expressed in symbols that make up scripts that predate our Latin alphabet by hundreds of years. Written rune symbols are called "staves." The runes are also called the "futhark" (and later due to language changes, "futhork"), which is the combination of the first six letters.

There are various proposed origins for runes because ancient evidence shows them spread across a wide geographic area. Norse legend says that the god Odin himself first discovered runes, but modern scholars believe that they were derived from an even earlier script, perhaps Etruscan in origin and blended with the ritual symbols of Teutonic shamans. Runes were used in the first or second century of the

Common Era by Germanic peoples, also known as Gothic, Suebian, or Teutonic peoples. Use of runes in modern times is not limited by ethnicity or nationality, and modern Germanic languages include Afrikaans, Flemish, Frisian, English, Gaelic, German, Icelandic, Norwegian, Swedish, and more. Claims of ancient runes discovered in North America were met with shock and renunciation by rune scholars. Modern-era runic systems such as Dalecarlian runes, the Runes of Honorius, and Witch's Runes have also been developed.

What little Scandinavian ancestry I have may not offer me a direct line to the ancient ones who used the first runes; nevertheless, I do find practical uses for these magical scripts. In fact, runes were my first "official" divination tools as a child, probably because stones and markers with which to make cheap and temporary rune stones are easy to come by. Divination is the art of telling fortunes with specialized tools and includes discovering past, present, and future knowledge. Runes are printed, painted, written, etched, or carved individually onto objects.

A collection of these objects that represent an entire runic alphabet, each with their own individual written rune, are sometimes called "trollrunes" (because trolls were associated with prophecy and magic), a set of runes, or simply runes. Ancient peoples may have used these runes for divination and magic. "Magic," to the ancient world and some modern practitioners, means creating change in one's world by using one's mind and spirit. Runes can act as a tool for magic and divination by allowing our minds to focus upon goals and probable outcomes. Because the runes were considered so sacred and might not have been used secularly, especially after their decline in use as a script, their use only in a sacred context now builds their power over time. It is believed magical symbols, used over and over again, can take on their own power in the collective human subconscious, much like how a wagon wheel wearing a rut in a road can make the path more evident and more easily traveled by that wagon over time.

How Can Runes Be Used?

A set of runes is a very useful thing to have, indeed. This divination tool can be used to discover the potential of your future career, love life, and more. They can help confirm your own personality traits and reveal which virtues you've yet to develop. Runes can empower you with advice about relationships, money, conflicts, and an infinite variety of topics. They can make predictions and destroy illusions. A set of runes can also be used as a powerful gateway to meditation, allowing you to take on blessings and banish negativity. Meditation is the practice of quieting or focusing the mind, and it is wonderful for relieving stress.

It's important to note that the runic stave symbols themselves can also be used alone, without a set of runes. I know that I'm introducing a lot of new terms here, but the distinctions are important. The overuse of the word "runes" confused me as a beginner. I could actually write the true statement that "you can paint runes on your runes to experience the power of the runes." I strive to use clarifying differentiation in this book to convert sentences like those into something like this: "You can paint staves on your rune stones to experience the power of the runes." I'll give you some concrete examples to help you understand.

Staves can be drawn on anything or anyone, even invisibly, and imbued with wishes to inspire and create change. They can also be used as a secret script to protect information. Staves can be carefully combined and even altered or invented to produce spiritual results. Just as we combine letters to make words, runes can be combined to enhance their meanings, sometimes by layering them on top of one another. Take care with runes. I once saw a man who had tattooed what he thought was an entire futhark, from beginning to end, on his arm just because it looked cool. I was concerned for him. That's not just harmless alphabet soup!

Like the Hebrew alphabet, staves have stand-alone sacred associations as well as the ability to spell out words. And because each runic letter not only has a phonetic meaning but also a spiritual meaning, imbuing random combinations of runes with spiritual power through ritual exercises such as tattooing is not advisable. There may be ancient wisdom contained in the order of runes in a runic alphabet. This book will give extensive instructions on how simple it is to use runes properly in divination and for spirituality.

Why Use Runes?

Divination is such a useful art. Fortune-telling is my regular job, five days a week. People come to me asking questions about choosing the right career, whether or not an old flame will be rekindled, and about the endless potential paths in life. I use divination in my personal life as well, often to help me refine and develop personality traits that can be both blessings and curses. Runes are so simple to make and to use that they make an excellent first divination tool. Some of the skills that are developed by using runes can easily transfer to the use of other divination tools, such as the tarot or fortune-telling cards. If you learn to divine with runes, you know that no matter what your situation in life may be, you will always have the means to empower yourself with sound advice.

Learning runes as a sacred script is valuable knowledge as well. You'll instantly have the power to draw a meditative focus on any object. You can bring the energy of success to your workplace and the power of protection and peace to your home. You'll have a secret script all your own that your family and colleagues won't be able to read even if it's emblazoned on your wall calendar. Rune-marked items even make wonderful gifts for others. And, once you're familiar with an entire runic alphabet, you may start to notice runes that others have hidden in plain sight. Now *that's* a super power.

How to Use This Book

Though this book is written for beginners, I've worked to make it a solid reference book for anyone's shelf. The true novice should work through the book from beginning to end, since I build one skill on top of another. From rote memorization of meanings, you'll move on toward simple interpretation and the myriad applications for runes, and you'll also learn advanced techniques that will help you make the runes your own.

Though I strive to use English words for techniques and concepts that span many cultures whenever possible, you'll find a glossary at the back of this book to help you learn some of the jargon. You'll also find, for your reference, helpful breakdowns of the phonetic sounds and meanings of the most commonly used runic alphabet (the Elder Futhark) in the first chapter. The third chapter is devoted to helpful diagrams and charts that allow you to use and interpret a set of runes to gather more precise knowledge on topics in your life that are important to you.

As you move through this book, it may be helpful to keep scrap paper handy to practice writing runes. I am more of a tactile learner than a visual one, which means I had to write down runic alphabets many times before they were committed to memory. I still need to practice writing obscure scripts in order to keep them fresh and accurate in my mind. It is safe to jot down runes in pencil on scratch paper in any combination for learning purposes. Just remember to treat runes with respect. Don't crumple up and abandon written runes just anywhere. Though I choose to burn my scratch paper that contains written runes, you can safely recycle or compost such paper. I suggest that you visualize their power melting harmlessly back into the earth as you add pieces of paper with staves written on them to the compost heap.

Prepare yourself for the spiritual disciplines of studious practice and plenty of memorization. The book you hold in your hands contains runes of power that will soon be yours to use. From A to Z, alphabets contain the means to create every sound within a language. Sounds and words bring forth human ideas into real manifestation, and thus they are truly divine. Speech is the breath of life that brings meaning to the connection between peoples across time and space. Handle the blessed runes, and all your words, with care.

one

Getting Started with Runes

By the time you finish this chapter, you should be able to get started with a simple rune reading. A "rune reading" is a divination session in which you ask the runes a question about your past, present, or future and receive an answer that you can interpret using the guides in this book. Learning through daily divination with runes is an effective way to memorize any runic alphabet. It is also a great way to discover information about your life, confirm what you already know, and empower yourself with advice on any topic under the sun.

Types of Runes

Here's a brief overview of runic alphabets to help you understand how rune meanings change over time. This factual information is important because otherwise it can be confusing to see one rune with two completely different meanings, when those meanings actually developed over a large span of time and geographic space.

I suggest that you only learn one runic alphabet at a time, otherwise it's pretty easy to mix them up. It is beyond the scope of this book to teach interpretations of all of the different runic alphabets. The different types of runes below are listed in alphabetical order. In this book I will thoroughly teach the use of only the first and oldest set of runes, the Elder Futhark. I've chosen this system as best for beginners because it is still the most popular in use and can easily be studied exclusively for an entire lifetime. The Elder Futhark system was one of the first I learned as a beginner, and it still serves me well to this day.

- *Anglo-Saxon Runes:* These runes expand on the original Elder Futhark row. This was probably done for writing, not for divination, in order to include more phonetic sounds as other peoples adopted runes as a means of writing. The Anglo-Saxon runes can include up to thirty-three characters. Though harder to memorize due to their number, these runes can add meanings to your lexicon. It would be best to learn these after learning the Elder Futhark.

- *Armanen Runes:* Though modern in origin, these were claimed to be the oldest runes in Nazi Germany, where the use of rune magic was perverted toward evil ends. Runes are a magical tool, and they can be misused. This dark time in history does not mean that runic alphabets, even the Armanen, are evil.

• *Dalecarlian Runes:* When Latin letters came into being, this runic system was an evolution of the Elder Futhark, Younger Futhark, and Medieval Runes, which changed markedly when they were mixed with several other alphabets. Again, this system is not used for divination.

• *Dotted Runes:* Dotted runes of the Viking Age expanded the Younger Futhark by adding dotted characters. This system was used as a script, not for divination.

• *Elder Futhark Runes:* These are the oldest runes and potentially the best place to start as a beginner. Not only are they the most common runes used for divination, but they will also help you learn other forms of runes that include Elder Futhark characters. The Elder Futhark runes are twenty-four in number. Much of this book will assume that you are using the Elder Futhark runes, though you can substitute other runes if you wish.

• *Frisian Runes:* These were one expansion of the Elder Futhark that included twenty-eight runes. This also marked the change of the word "futhark" to "futhork" because of the introduction of a new fourth rune that changed the sound.

• *Gothic Runes:* The Goths, Northern European peoples, adopted the use of runic script of twenty-five characters. Gothic runes can be used for divination. These brought in influences from Greek deities.

- *Marcomannic Runes:* These runes are a mixture of Elder Futhark and Anglo-Saxon runes. Though historically interesting, there's no particular reason to learn the Marcomannic runes for divination unless you really like the meanings of the runes that are included. There are twenty-nine of these runes.

- *Medieval Runes:* These runes are a version of the Younger Futhark that were re-expanded to include more sounds. Though they are of historical and magical interest, these are not commonly used for divination.

- *Runes of Honorius:* Also called Theban, this script is not technically runic at all, nor is it commonly used for divination. Nevertheless, it is used as a sacred script. Written words can be charged with energy in a method similar to runes that is explained in the fourth chapter of this book.

- *Witch's Runes:* A modern invention, Witch's Runes are purely divinatory and not a script. Though there are several variations, they typically consist of thirteen pictograms. Since the pictograms are more meaningful than the simple lines of old runic alphabets, I've found these to be much easier to memorize and a good option for beginners or children who are struggling to learn. Still, they are quite useful for advanced practitioners. The version I use is detailed in *A Witch's Runes: How to Make and Use Your Own Magick Stones* by Susan Sheppard.

- *Younger Futhark Runes:* These Scandinavian runes evolved due to historical changes in language use and actually have fewer characters. Some of the runes took on additional sounds and eliminated the necessity for the full set of characters. Since there are only sixteen of them, the Younger Futhark runes are a good option for those who are struggling to learn the Elder Futhark runes. Step back and just learn the Younger Futhark runes first, if this is the case, and then expand your knowledge to the Elder Futhark later on. There are long-branch, short-branch, and staveless (meaning they lack certain strokes) and stylistic variations of these runes. Use the long-branch. The short-branch and staveless are useless for divination due to the impossibility of telling whether you're reading some characters right-side up or upside down.

Learning What They Mean

Learning what runes mean begins as a practice of rote memorization because the runes don't give you many clues by their shape. Originally, the runes were developed to resemble things like the horns of a now-extinct species of ox and other objects we no longer see in everyday life. One rune is often similar to another, being either straight-lined or zigzag in shape. So you'll have to be gentle with yourself and allow yourself time to learn. As a child it may have taken you years to master the alphabet for your own language. Be patient. Perhaps the easiest form of runes to memorize is the Witch's Runes because they're pictograms that represent their meanings and because they're so few in number. The hardest of the divination scripts for me to memorize was the ogham, which will be explained in chapter 2, because the letters all look very similar. Again, I suggest you begin with the Elder Futhark. You can make some flash cards out of three-by-five-inch notecards. I find it much easier to first associate each runic letter with its divination meaning than to try to memorize pronunciation, name, and symbolic meaning all at once.

Understanding the Elder Futhark

The Elder Futhark is organized into groups, each called a "family" (*aett*), of eight in order. The Elder Futhark, the most commonly used runes, is divided into three aetts of eight. The first, starting with fehu and ending with wunjo, is ruled by fertility gods and is called "Freya's Eight." The second is called "Hagall's Eight," starting with hagalaz and ending with sowilo, and is ruled by protection deities. The third is called "Tyr's Eight," starting with tiwaz and ending with dagaz, and is ruled by deities of divine justice and order.

A blank rune named "wyrd" or "Odin" does not fit into any of the aettir. The blank rune is a modern addition and entirely optional, by the way. I don't personally use it. If you write out the Elder Futhark runes in these three sets of eight, it may help you organize similar meanings in groups in your mind. The eights are also useful for hiding runes in code, which will be explained in the section about hidden runes in chapter 6.

I fully intend to help the beginner memorize these runes, so I've kept my explanations of them focused on that goal. For each of the Elder Futhark runes, you will be given information on name, number, name pronunciation, phonetic sound, imagery, and interpretation.

- *Rune Name:* Since the runes varied across region and time periods, some of them have varied names. I've selected one name with a pronunciation guide so that the beginner can have a consistent and complete system, but be aware that there may be more names out there to investigate. Check out the recommended reading guide at the end of this book.

• *Rune Number:* The order of the futhark is vital. The order of the runes can help you memorize them in the same way that you learned the alphabet with the alphabet song. The number can also be used for numerology or in rune readings when you are trying to get a number in the form of a calendar date, age, or dollar amount.

• *Suggested Pronunciation:* Singing rune names while cutting runes, meditating, or casting spells may have been an ancient practice. For this reason I'll include a suggested pronunciation for each rune's name. There may be several different ways to pronounce each rune. I chose pronunciations that are simple for a beginner and, whenever possible, can help you remember a rune's meaning and sound.

• *Sounds Like:* Knowledge of the phonetic sound is vital if you're going to use or interpret staves as a script. The singing or chanting of runes may have been done using only their phonetic sound as well, adding another use for phonetic knowledge. Learning the phonetic sound may allow you to discern names of people in the runes during a reading.

• *Visualize:* As a beginner, all staves can look alike! I'll give you some mental pictures to assign to each rune. These are from the traditional meanings, modern meanings, and some of my own personal imaginings, so pick whatever imagery works for you to help match the rune stave with its meaning. Visualize that mental picture overlaid on the stave to give meaning to your runes.

• *Remember:* This will be a list of interpretations for the rune. Whenever possible, I've tried to stick with words that match the sound of the rune. This is a mnemonic device to help you memorize the interpretations and rune sounds because, at first, reading runes will involve rote memorization for the beginner. You'll integrate some more words and understandings in your own mind as you go along, and that's great, even if they don't fit with my alliteration pattern.

The Elder Futhark Runes

Fehu

Rune Number: 1

Suggested Pronunciation: FAY-hoo

Sounds Like: F as in "fee"

Visualize: Ancient peoples imagined *fehu* as representing cattle, the source of most of their food and clothing. Visualize this stave as a lone, standing cow who still has her short horns jutting out as she looks right, toward the future. Of course, the stave also looks a little like the letter F, which can help you remember its sound.

Since this is the first rune in the futhark, it can often mean beginnings.

Remember: Fortune, fee, fief, feudal, Freyr, fire, fertility, fitness

Uruz

Rune Number: 2

Suggested Pronunciation: oo-ROOZ

Sounds Like: U as in "ukulele"

Visualize: *Uruz* referred to a wild horned ox that is now extinct. Its horns sat low on its head and curved forward, almost down rather than up. Visualize the uruz stave as a strong ox with his head bowed down, ready to push back against any odds. Later, the uruz rune became associated with a rainstorm. Now visualize the uruz stave as a cloud with a strong downspout of rain pouring down upon the earth. Try to associate one of these visualizations with the interpretation of uruz, or invent your own imagery that works for you.

Remember: Oomph, useful, utensil, use

Thurisaz

Rune Number: 3

Suggested Pronunciation: THOOR-ee-sahz

Sounds Like: Th

Visualize: Early on, the *thurisaz* rune was thought to be a giant. Imagine the thurisaz stave as a fearsome ax carried by a giant monster. Later, people imagined thurisaz as a thorn. Now visualize the thurisaz stave as a thorn jutting out from the side of a plant's stem. Use whichever visualization helps you remember the meanings below, or make up one of your own.

Remember: Thorn, Thor's hammer, thistle

Ansuz

Rune Number: 4

Suggested Pronunciation: AHN-sooz

Sounds Like: Ah

Visualize: Imagine the *ansuz* stave as a magical staff of the god Odin with the light of blessings shining down from it onto the people below.

Remember: Authority, ancestors, advice, ash tree, air, active, assurance

Raido

Rune Number: 5

Suggested Pronunciation: RYE-thoh

Sounds Like: R

Visualize: *Raido* represents the chariot that the god Thor drives across the skies to make the sounds of thunder. Visualize the raido stave as a chariot. If I use my imagination, I can see it as an unhitched chariot pointing to the right. Of course, it also looks much more like the letter R, which can help you remember some of these alliterative interpretations.

Remember: Riding, rhythm, ritual, rolling along, road trip, realization, result, rethinking, right, restlessness

Ken

Rune Number: 6

Suggested Pronunciation: KEHN

Sounds Like: K

Visualize: At first *ken* represented a torch. Visualize the stave as a torch jutting off a castle wall with the flame licking up toward the wall to think about the illuminating capabilities of ken. Later on, the rune took on a new meaning: ulcer. It can be gross to imagine the indentation of the stave as a wound, but this is one option for remembering the healing properties of ken.

Remember: Kismet, controlled healing, comprehension, command, cunning, compassion, conclusion

Gebo

Rune Number: 7

Suggested Pronunciation: GIFF-oo

Sounds Like: G as in "gift"

Visualize: I like to imagine *gebo* as the above view of a gift wrapped in a ribbon and left at my feet. It also represents a partnership, so you can visualize hands shaking or think of it as the symbol for kisses you might leave at the end of a letter.

Remember: Gift, good bargain, guarantee, grant, gratitude, giving

Wunjo

Rune Number: 8

Suggested Pronunciation: WOON-yoh

Sounds Like: W

Visualize: Imagine climbing to the top of a mountain and planting your *wunjo*-shaped flag. Wunjo is the ecstatic joy of success.

Remember: Wonderful, winning

Hagalaz

Rune Number: 9

Suggested Pronunciation: HAH-gah-lahz

Sounds Like: H

Visualize: *Hagalaz* looks like H, which shares its sound. It also represents a hailstorm, so since "hail" starts with H, this can help you remember its meaning. Think of the two straight lines as hailstones falling down and the crossbar as a jagged, angry lightning streak across the sky.

Remember: Hail, horrible, havoc, hex, happenstance, hardship, harm, hell, hostility

Neid

Rune Number: 10

Suggested Pronunciation: NYED (rhymes with "vied")

Sounds Like: N as in "need"

Visualize: Visualize the *neid* stave as crossed kindling for a fire. When you are cold, you must seek warmth. This symbolizes how the need-fire burns within all of us when we are striving to protect and preserve ourselves and our deepest desires.

Remember: Need, need-fire, necessity, neglected, needy

Isa

Rune Number: 11

Suggested Pronunciation: EES

Sounds Like: E as in "sleep"

Visualize: Picture an icicle hanging from a rooftop. *Isa* represents the cold, hard barrier that ice creates when it blocks forward motion.

Remember: Impediment, eerie stillness, eternity, intent, inability, evasiveness, inaction

Jera

Rune Number: 12

Suggested Pronunciation: YEHR-ah

Sounds Like: J as in "journey" but also Y as in "year," since Germanic languages often used (and still use) the letter J to represent a Y sound

Visualize: To me, the *jera* stave looks like a winding path. This represents the time and effort that it takes to reap good rewards.

Remember: Yes, year's wages, yours, jump, journey, joy, justice, germination, generosity

Eihwaz

Rune Number: 13

Suggested Pronunciation: EYE-wahz

Sounds Like: An uncertain vowel sound lost to past dialects, possibly sounding like "eye." Some pronounce it somewhere between an E and an I.

Visualize: The ancient people visualized a yew tree with the *eihwaz* rune because the yew was what was used to make a bow to shoot arrows. You can imagine the stave as a tree with roots as large as its canopy. Some believe that this tree is the world tree, from which all existence flows.

Remember: Adaptability, analytical, endurance, enlightenment, empowerment, renunciation

Pertho

Rune Number: 14

Suggested Pronunciation: PEHR-thoh

Sounds Like: P

Visualize: Imagine a dice cup being thrown to the right with two dice flying out. Or visualize *pertho* as the cauldron of death and rebirth stirred by life, yet it has been tipped on its side so that anything can happen.

Remember: Possibility, pleasure, predestination, precognition, providence, procreation, plain to see, poetic, profane, playfulness, perversion

Algiz

Rune Number: 15

Suggested Pronunciation: ahl-GHEEZ

Sounds Like: Originally this rune sounded like a Z, but it soon developed into an R sound in some dialects.

Visualize: The stave of *algiz* looks like the antlers of an elk. The antlers protect that elk, and so too algiz can protect you and keep you calm and peaceful in the face of danger.

Remember: Zen, zapping your enemies, refuge, reassurance, reliability, repel, refusal

Sowilo

Rune Number: 16

Suggested Pronunciation: soh-WEE-loh

Sounds Like: S as in "sun"

Visualize: A lightning bolt or a ray of sunshine streams down from the sky, warming you with life-giving energy. This is *sowilo*.

Remember: Sun, success, sustenance, security, salary, safety, stroke of luck, soul, stress, strength, self-confidence, steadfastness, style

Tiwaz

Rune Number: 17

Suggested Pronunciation: TEE-wahz

Sounds Like: T as in "Tuesday"

Visualize: *Tiwaz* is the spear held by the war god Tyr. Visualize the stave as a spear, or as the straight and narrow path on which all that is just and true will be revealed as long as you follow the rules.

Remember: Tyr, Tuesday, triumph, tribute, truth, trial, tribunal, tests

Berkanan

Rune Number: 18

Suggested Pronunciation: BEHR-kahn-ahn

Sounds Like: B

Visualize: The *berkanan* stave looks very much like the letter B that shares its sound. It is a nurturing rune, so visualize its stave as the side view of a pregnant woman or as a woman's-eye view of her own breasts.

Remember: Birch twig, birth, babies, breasts, beautiful woman, bear

Ehwaz

Rune Number: 19

Suggested Pronunciation: AY-wahz

Sounds Like: E as in "expedition"

Visualize: The stave for *ehwaz* originally represented a horse, so imagine it as a profile view of a horse. In those times, horses were used for travel. Just as the cooperation and loyalty between humans and horses can build civilization, the partnership represented by ehwaz can also mean marriage and controlling oneself in relationships.

Remember: Equine, expedition, enterprise, experimental, accord, affinity for another, alliance, advancing, adornments, agent, association with others

Mannaz

Rune Number: 20

Suggested Pronunciation: MAHN-ahz

Sounds Like: M as in "mankind"

Visualize: This rune can be imagined as a man standing in the space in the middle of the rune holding two axes, one at each of his sides. I often imagine it as a man looking into a mirror. This rune can represent all of mankind or just one male person in a reading.

Remember: Mankind, members of your family, memory, memories, mental pursuits, mind, mindfulness, magician, mysticism, microcosm, man, male

Laguz

Rune Number: 21

Suggested Pronunciation: LAH-ghooz

Sounds Like: L as in "life"

Visualize: The stave for *laguz* looks like a rotated L that now represents its sound. (I knew that my dyslexia would come in handy someday.) It can also represent a pint of beer with a leek hanging out of it, which was a Norse protective charm to prevent the drinker from becoming poisoned. Laguz represents imaginative use of creativity. It might even represent the magnificently carved wooden prow of a Viking boat because laguz can mean a journey across water. As always, you can choose your own imagery to help you remember laguz.

Remember: Lagoon, lake, life, love, looking into the future

Ingwaz

Rune Number: 22

Suggested Pronunciation: ING-wahz

Sounds Like: A nasal N or NG as in "loving"

Visualize: Imagine an arrow coming out of the page straight at you. Looking at the tip, all you would see is *ingwaz*. That's because this rune represents this moment in time. Since the spark of creativity is in this moment, ingwaz represents conception and can thus also be visualized as a vagina or the tip of a phallus.

Remember: Now, nervous energy, natal, nurturing, nourishing, entrance

Othila

Rune Number: 23

Suggested Pronunciation: OH-thee-LAH

Sounds Like: O as in "home"

Visualize: The stave for *othila* vaguely looks like a loop, the line coming around to meet in the middle. This represents the home because it shows the journey away from home and back again. Moreover, the idea of home can expand to mean ancestral property or inheritance. Reincarnation, as some ancient and modern people believe, will lead us back home again to our soul family.

Remember: Oasis, obituaries, owner, origins, owed, old country

Dagaz

Rune Number: 24

Suggested Pronunciation: DAH-ghaz

Sounds Like: D

Visualize: The *dagaz* stave looks like an infinity symbol. To me, it also looks like two letter Ds mirroring one another, which reminds me of the words "dawn" and "dusk."

Since this is the last letter in the futhark, it can mean endings, which is interesting because it can also mean new beginnings. Every beginning is an ending and vice versa.

Remember: Day, destiny, dawn, daylight, dusk, darkness, death, dedication, development, defining, disillusionment

The Blank Rune

Rune Number: (Not applicable)

Pronunciation: Some people call this the "wyrd rune" or the "Odin rune."

Sounds Like: (Not applicable)

Visualize: A blank rune can often be included in a rune set as a visual reminder of the mystery of the unknown. This rune is entirely optional.

Remember: Unknowable, void, it's in the hands of the gods

What You Need for Reading and Interpreting Runes

You'll need a set of runes and a bag in which to keep your runes and to use during some forms of the divination. You'll also need a comfortable space to do your rune readings. Some people need privacy to be able to perform divination comfortably, especially as beginners. You will need to have a space without distractions such as electronics, people, and noise. You may need a flat surface for some rune-reading techniques and, of course, good lighting to be able to see your runes.

I also highly recommend that you write down the results of your divination. Sometimes a rune won't make sense to you in the context of the question you've asked, but it will make a lot more sense at some later time. As a teenager I would draw runes for conflict before breakups with my high school boyfriends. The rune didn't make sense until after the breakup happened, since I was generally socially clueless that the relationship drama was about to occur. You might also discover patterns by recording the results of your rune readings. A friend of mine told me today that she had pulled a rune representing rebirth four times in the last week during a daily random drawing from her rune set. That sort of random happenstance is considered significant because it's statistically rare, but it may be difficult to detect unless you're keeping meticulous records.

You can buy sets of runes or make your own. Some people believe that runes received as a gift are better than runes that are purchased. I've purchased sets of runes and made my own, and I don't find any difference in accuracy or precision between the two. However, the runes I've made feel more special and spiritually significant when I use them, and this feeling increases the longer I keep them and use them.

Pulling a Rune in Daily Divination and Meditative Practice

The best way to memorize runes is through practice, practice, practice. That means that you should be laying your eyes on at least one rune every day. I suggest pulling a "rune of the day" from your bag and writing it down in a journal. Look up the meaning of that rune and write it down next to the rune. Then, start freely associating what you think that rune might mean for you on this day. For example, if a rune represents birth, it would of course be meaningful if you were a pregnant woman ready to give birth. However, it could also be meaningful if you were about to start painting a picture, thus giving creative birth to an art project. Write down the date and your initial thoughts. Leave some space to add writing later if that rune's meaning becomes more apparent to you later in the day, week, or month. When you've run out of ideas for that rune, simply gaze at it for a few moments of meditation, imprinting its shape and meaning in your mind.

This process is repetitive for a reason. It will help you build your memorization and create associations with runes in your everyday life. For this reason, your date with the runes each day should become a priority. Try writing it down on your to-do list, setting a reminder alarm on your electronic devices, or building it into your morning or bedtime routine. You'll notice that you become quicker at the process as you go, and that's a good thing. Your daily rune will eventually become a welcome break in your day and an opportunity to see the future coming and add spiritual meaning to an otherwise ordinary day.

To create a lasting rune journal, I suggest getting a binder to insert your notes. This way, you can add to each individual rune's meanings and interpretations as your experience with your runes grows. I find that, during some periods of my life, I'll draw the same rune again and again. Repeat runes happen so that you can learn how the meaning applies to your life. You might have an initial interpretation from the book, such as the rune algiz meaning protection. However, in a few days if you experienced a car accident and then the next time you pull algiz you run out of gas on the highway, the rune begins to take on the more specific meaning that you need to protect yourself from car troubles. The third time you pull that rune and check your journal, you're likely to take your car in for a tune-up and make sure that you check the oil, gas, and tires before you go anywhere. Each rune set can take on its own specific language for you so that getting to know a new set of runes is like getting to know a new friend.

Runic Dance: Runic Yoga for Body Divination and Rune Memorization

To get the creative juices flowing, some people use full body movements to connect with the runes, calling this practice "runic dance" or "runic yoga." Getting your body moving to stimulate learning and inspiration is something that I was taught when I was earning my master's degree in teaching. It's often not enough for a science student, for example, to learn the motions of the planets or of the electrons by looking at pictures or words on a page; she might have to get up out of her seat and orbit the room like a planet or electron herself. Kinetic learners, those who learn by moving and doing things, will benefit from some of these meditative exercises.

Runic movements are usually done by assuming a body pose that at least vaguely resembles a rune. For example, to pose like isa you would stand straight with your arms flat to your side. Some people choose to slowly turn in a circle while intoning the sound of the rune, in this case singing the I vowel, before moving on to the next rune pose. There are books devoted to rune yoga, with specific examples, but because this book is for beginners and encourages creativity, I suggest that you use your visualization skills to assume the poses as they fit your own body instead of trying to conform to diagrams or pictures of other peoples' contortions.

To gain further familiarity with the runes, you can dance the runes each in turn from the beginning of the runic alphabet to the end. If you're doing a spiritual exercise with a knowing, bindrune, or rune wheel, you can just dance each of the runes involved and leave out the rest. I've used rune dance to help me remember tricky rune meanings that keep slipping my mind by meditating upon the meaning of a rune while assuming the pose and visualizing my body taking the shape of the stave. I've also used runic dance to help puzzle out what a reading means when divination has me stumped. For example, if I'm worried about how hagalaz might apply to my relationship in a relationship reading, I can dance hagalaz and breathe its name while pushing all other thoughts from my mind. The meanings that come to me may be new and more profound when trying to embody the rune than they would be if I simply looked up more meanings for the rune that others have developed.

Ritual Meditation Dedication Ceremony

Doing a daily meditation on each rune in succession over the course of a month can be one way to memorize the runes and also can feel like a bit of a journey, so I've decided to combine the process of memorizing them with a little ceremony and celebration. This can help you dedicate yourself as a practitioner of runic divination and magic. There are many words and titles for one who uses runes. One of the most common is "runemaster" and the modern feminine "runemistress." I personally like the gender-ambiguous Old English terms *runa* or *runwita,* meaning a wise or cunning person. The latter sounds related to the word "witch," and after this dedication ritual, you can consider yourself a rune witch, in a sense. You can also use the meditation part of this exercise, omitting the bread making, to make a set of runes or dedicate a completed set to your rune work.

The idea of this ritual is that you will meditate on a rune while intoning its sound and forming your hands into a rough shape of the rune. Then you will eat a piece of herbal rune bread that has been dedicated to that rune, taking the runic energies inside you. The first step will be preparing the bread for your journey through the runes. Meditate upon each rune in order, from the start of the alphabet to its end. You can perform this entire dedication in as few as twenty-four days if you use the Elder Futhark, excluding the optional blank rune of mystery at the end. It is okay to spread it out over more days if needed. It was designed to be performed within the span of a month. If you use a shorter runic system such as the Witch's Runes, begin when the moon is just beginning to be a waxing sliver and then ride on that moon's waxing energy until it is full or very nearly full.

Here is the bread recipe. You'll want to make at least two loaves to have enough slices. You can make them ahead of time and slice and freeze some of the bread, or bake loaves as you go along as needed. This recipe makes use of some commonly available herbs that are associated with some of the runes.

Rune Bread

4 cups water

A bag of chamomile tea for success from sowilo

3 tablespoons honey

Yeast (1 packet or 2¼ teaspoons)

3 cups flour of your choice

3 tablespoons oil

3 pinches salt

3 tablespoons pine nuts (ground or whole) for inspiration from ken

3 tablespoons flax seeds (ground or whole) for joy from
wunjo

A sprinkling of rosemary to taste to help your rune practice
pay off with jera

Make chamomile tea by boiling 4 cups of water and adding
the tea bag. Wait until the tea has cooled to a pleasant warm
temperature. Place 1 tablespoon of honey and the yeast in a
measuring cup, and add about ½–1 cup warm tea to proof the
yeast while you mix the other ingredients. Leave room in your
measuring cup for the mixture to potentially double in size.

Grab a mixing bowl and add the oil first. It helps keep the
bread from sticking too much to the sides. Mix together the
salt, pine nuts, flax seeds, and rosemary in the mixing bowl
with a fork. When the yeast has doubled in size, mix it in
with the dry ingredients. Add chamomile tea 1 cup at a time
until the dough reaches the right consistency; it should be
pliable but firm. You might not use all of the tea. Knead it until mixed and then let the dough rest for 90 minutes. Punch
down the dough and put it in a greased loaf pan for another
60 minutes. Bake at 375°F for about 30 minutes or until the
crust is golden brown. Makes 1 loaf.

Alternative Option

If your diet doesn't allow for any kind of bread, consider using apple slices instead. It is easy to carve runes into them,
and they hold the energy of ingwaz, which represents all of
the potential of the moment of now. This single rune holds
the nascent energy from which all other energies can follow.
Some other runic foods you can add to make a rune feast is

stinging nettle tea, to drink in the success energy of fehu, and a side of leeks, to take in the divination power of laguz.

Ritual Steps: One Rune per Day

Step 1: Gather your bread, a knife, and any runic objects you wish to consecrate. You may wish to toast the bread beforehand. Optionally you can bring your favorite bread spread and a glass of water (or chamomile or nettle tea) to wash it down.

Step 2: Create sacred space. You can do this by locking the doors and turning off distracting electronics, lighting a candle, burning your favorite incense, or playing music that puts you in the mood. You might choose to go out in nature and use a natural setting as sacred space.

Step 3: Lay a slice of the bread in front of you. Carve the stave of the rune of the day into the bread. You can use your favorite spread on the bread instead, but some believe that the act of ritually cutting the rune gives this process more power. You can toast the bread first and scratch the rune into it if you want to make the rune more visible.

Step 4: Hold your hands over the rune in roughly the shape of the rune. This is called making a mudra and is used in rune meditation in order to attune to the rune's energy.

Step 5: Keeping your hand held over the rune, chant or sing the rune's sound. Some choose to chant the name of the rune, while others choose the phonetic sound (a rune like sowilo would just be a hiss). We know the runes were traditionally sung, but we don't know for sure which option the ancients used. I suggest the beginner choose to sing the phonetic sound because the knowledge of the runes' sounds can be useful for divination of names or other words that are sounded out from the staves. If it is runic magic that interests you more, chant the rune name, as rune name chants can be used in runic magic to good effect. Your meditation can last twenty minutes ideally, but if you are unaccustomed to meditation, it's okay if this step is a lot shorter than that.

Step 6: Eat the bread, visualizing the rune's energy becoming a part of you.

Step 7: Give thanks to the rune or to the divine for teaching you. Extinguish any candles and rest a moment to allow yourself to return to the mundane world, or go to bed as soon as possible and record your dreams when you awaken for messages from that rune.

Divination with Runes:
Casts, Charts, and Spreads

There are many ways to get prepared for reading runes. In this chapter I'll be sharing a lot of different exercises to do before, during, and after rune reading. Don't be confused if you notice that some steps seem to overlap or to be mutually exclusive. The point here is to give you lots of tools for your tool belt. You can choose which way you want to do things according to how practical and comfortable the style of rune reading fits into your life. Pick one way and stick with it, or cycle through different methods to find one that matches your personality and goals.

Getting Ready

First, get into the right frame of mind or settle on a philosophy about your use of the runes that aids your ability to use them with the frequency you desire. Many beginners lack confidence. They worry that they do not have what it takes to be an excellent fortune-teller. In ancient times, however, divination wasn't some sort of special gift of psychic abilities. Using runes was something that every head of the household may have done on a regular basis. Ancient peoples thought of themselves as a conduit for the knowledge handed down from their gods. So relax and let the information flow through you as you learn with your runes.

When I worked as a schoolteacher at a new school, I could easily fit runes into my everyday life. I didn't do much special preparation. I sought out privacy by choice and all I needed was my runes, a bag, and a surface. It's okay to wait until the timing is lucky for a reading. A full moon is a great time for a reading because one's intuitive abilities are heightened. Some avoid reading when the moon is dark or void-of-course, taking this as a time for resting psychic energies. Since fortune-telling is now my full-time day job, I obviously don't wait for special occasions or avoid using runes during unfavorable times, but a beginner can certainly experiment to see whether the moon's activity significantly affects reading ability. Many people pull a rune out of the bag before divination just for a "yes" or "no" answer to whether divination should take place. If the rune is generally negative in nature, it means to try again later. If the rune is positive, it's a sign to go ahead with the reading. For the beginner, more preparation before a reading might get you in the right headspace and help you make rune reading more of a special moment, if that's what you choose to do.

If you'd like to do some more preparation, here are some things that I like to do in order to add some atmosphere to a rune reading. Background music like soft drumming or meditative instrumentals are optional. I like to light some incense and do rune readings by soft candlelight. Since I paint or carve staves that contrast with their background, I don't need bright lighting to see my runes like I might in a palm reading or a tea-leaf reading, so rune readings are a good excuse for soft lighting. I can let my eyes lose focus and just relax into the intuition of the moment.

Clearing out negative spiritual energy that fills the air is another way to prepare for a rune reading. It's a way to ensure that the readings remain unaffected by negativity. People do this in many ways, perhaps by lighting a sage smudge stick and wafting it around or by sweeping the space with a broom. Some people think that mischievous spirits can influence your runes if this step is not observed, but I don't worry about that too much. The way negativity affects me is when the problems of the outside world start ruining my ability to focus on my runes. If I'm thinking about how I should be working on my dissertation and have to keep arguing with myself about how moderation, breaks, and focusing on my spirituality with runes is important, I won't be in the right headspace. Clearing out the negative energy of my daily stress is a useful step in preparing for a reading.

Next, bless the space or energetically shield and protect it in order to fill the void you just created by clearing the space. I like to draw a circle around myself with my hand in order to keep in all the positive energies that I'm working with in my rune reading. You can add salt to water and sprinkle this "holy water" around to bless the area, light some of your favorite incense, or simply take some time to pray or meditate for a moment, focusing on positive feelings. If you want to add more ritual to your readings, you are free to do so. And you can certainly omit elaborate preparations if that's more your speed. We don't know exactly how ancient peoples prepared to use runes for divination, so you can create your own modern traditions for yourself.

Runecasts: Casting Patterns

A runecast is one simple way to read the runes. This method is one that I originally learned by casting unmarked bones. As a beginner, it may help for you to practice with unmarked bones as well before adding the rune symbol interpretations to the mix. You can dry out chicken bones for this purpose. I collected old cattle bones found in the desert for this purpose, since I'm a vegetarian. I also ask my meat-eating friends and family to save wishbones for this and other magical purposes.

Take your runes or bones or stones and cast them out of a bag onto a flat surface. I like to cast them on the ground and then stand up to get a good look at them from a distance, but if you prefer to be seated and cast them onto a table, that is okay too. You'll notice that some naturally fall closer to each other in clusters and some naturally fall farther away. If you used runes, this means that the runes in clusters are the heart of the situation and are related to one another. If you used unmarked bones or stones, you'll look for specific patterns.

Some common arrangements are triangles, squares, circles, lines, and arrows. Here are the meanings of these patterns as they work for me. You'll probably notice new patterns or assign some new meanings. Be sure to write these down in your rune journal.

- *Arrow:* When pointing to the left, it means to look toward the past. When pointing to the right, the reading refers to the future. When the arrow points up, it means that the situation is evolving or the problem will be transcended. When the arrow points down, it means a major setback.

- *Cross:* A cross indicates tension and conflict. The runes that make up each arm of the cross might each represent a different aspect of the issue at hand. Note that one arm of the cross may dominate by being longer than the others.

- *Line:* If the runes are marked, a line can show the progression of a situation from one rune to another. Read them in order as if you were reading words on a page. If you are using unmarked bones or stones, a line can represent a blockage, so look for other patterns on both sides of the line to see what is being blocked.

- *Triangle:* A triangle is a good sign showing harmony and balance. It represents strength and forward motion.

- *Square:* A square represents stability, money, and staying in one place.

- *Circle:* A circle can represent protection, relationships, and love.

Even more patterns can be gleaned from studying astrology, wherein the patterns of the planets in the sky at the time of one's birth can be assessed for personality characteristics. The scattered random patterns of planets in the sky, or in this case runes on a cloth, and their adapted meanings as I use them are summarized below.

- *Bowl:* All of the runes are scattered on one half of the diagram or casting surface or form a shape in their pattern like a half-circle or the cross-section of a bowl wherever you've cast them. This shows that the subject is of a divided mind or is closed-off to one way of seeing or doing things. This pattern can also mean that a person shows one side of himself or herself but not the other.

- *Bucket:* This pattern looks identical to the bowl except that it has one outlier—the rune that represents the handle of the bucket. The outlier rune then becomes a focus of the reading that draws all of the other runes in the bucket together.

- *Bundle:* The runes seem to all be constrained to about a third of the diagram or casting surface, leaving the rest entirely clear. This means that the subject of the reading is limited, is feeling trapped, or has intentionally withdrawn from the situation.

- *Sling:* Same as the bowl pattern except with one outlier rune that represents the handle of the sling, like the handle on the Big Dipper constellation. The lone rune represents a single-minded focus of the subject of the reading.

- *Splash:* When the runes seem evenly and randomly scattered around the casting surface, this is interpreted as a lack of a sense of purpose or direction on the part of the person for whom the reading is done.
- *Splay:* Runes appear in small and closely-clumped groups placed evenly throughout the reading surface. The splay pattern shows that the subject of the reading has boldly independent interests and will not be turned aside from his or her goals.

When using runes, you can begin to build upon these meanings with the staves you see. Don't read the runes that are facedown on the surface. Those runes represent unexpressed potential and thus are not pertinent to the reading. Runes with unexpressed potential can be used in readings in which you are seeking out options you've not yet explored, like if you were trying to figure out whether a love interest that hasn't yet entered your life is better than two current love interests. But, for most beginner readings, facedown runes can be safely ignored as not applicable. They do count toward making up the pattern of the runes, even if their meanings are not read, just as the choices you don't make still affect your life. An exception to not reading facedown runes is if you choose to use a blank rune in your reading as a means of indicating that runes near it are also the crux of the situation. In this case, you'll have to peek under each overturned rune until you discover which one is the blank rune.

Take stock of which runes are clustered together to make the smallest patterns first, as they are the heart of the matter. For example, if a cluster falls in a circle, the runes may represent people involved in a relationship together. If the cluster falls in a square, the runes showing in that square may pertain to a business or workplace. If there are runes showing in an arrow pointing to the right, these runes reveal the future.

Rune casting for reading patterns is an excellent technique to use for general readings in order to allow the runes to tell you what you should be focusing on in your life right now. However, many people who use runes for divination already have a specific question in mind when they come to the runes. Whether it's about love or money, the past or the future, it can test one's patience to do a reading that insists upon giving you messages on topics other than the one that holds your attention.

I remember as a young college student casting the runes over and over again with a crumbling relationship in mind and being frustrated that they were giving me messages about my academics, family, and career path instead. It's as if the runes were telling me by omission that the relationship was done and that I needed to move on and turn my attention to other things. After all, the overturned runes were unexpressed potential, and those runes that might pertain to my love life remained firmly facedown. Sometimes allowing these freeform readings even when you have a specific topic in mind can be a good thing. It means that the runes take on a life of their own to give you spiritual guidance, telling you the messages you need to know instead of telling you what you want to hear. However, there is a solution if you want the runes to give you a little more precision in your readings: the use of a rune chart.

Rune Charts

A rune chart is a diagram on a surface upon which you cast the runes. It allows you to divine additional meanings from the place where the runes fall on the chart. An example of a rune chart that you might possibly have lying around the house is a Ouija board. A Ouija board is a spirit board upon which all the letters of the alphabet, the single digit numbers, and the words "yes" and "no" are printed. You can make your own on a piece of paper. Omit the planchette, which is the device used to indicate the symbols on the board. Cast runes onto the board instead to perform a spirit reading with runes. If you make a special set of black runes used only for spirit communication purposes, it can be used to speak with a group of ancestors. The runes that fall upright on letters may represent the first initial of an ancestor coming forward. Runes that fall on "yes" and "no" may indicate their advice for you. Runes that fall on numbers can answer questions about dates in time or any other numerical question.

There are many rune charts in use already out there, and you can make your own suited to your purpose. In fact, you can make a rune chart for just a single question. For example, if a woman is struggling to choose between two handsome suitors, she can write the names of each lover on a piece of paper and then cast the runes upon the paper to compare which man would be best for her by the runes that fall on or near his name. Rune charts that I've designed for many different purposes will be in chapter 3 under each common topic's subheading, so you can look them up according to what reading question is on your mind. A common rune chart that can be used for any topic is Finn's Window.

Finn's Window

The rune chart and rune-casting technique called Finn's Window is my favorite because it combines some magical technique, some stone- or bone-casting traditional knowledge, and rune-reading methods. One must start by using a rune chart that is emblazoned upon a surface. This could be a cloth with the design written on it, lines drawn in the dirt on the ground, or a painted table. Finn's Window is simply a circle that is divided into quarters by crosshairs. The size of Finn's Window depends on the size of your runes. All of the runes should be able to fit easily within the circle with plenty of space so that you can see whether some runes are clustering closer together.

For Finn's Window to be done properly, you'll also need a symbolic object associated with your question. For example, if you are trying to speak to your deceased grandmother, you might want to use a pair of her eyeglasses. (You might want to toss the runes gently if you are using breakable objects, though I've never damaged anything with my favorite wooden runes.) If you wish to perform a reading for your sister, you might use a lock of her hair. If you're hoping to have a baby, you might draw a picture of a pregnant woman. For a reading on your marriage, use your wedding rings. Place the object or objects in the middle of Finn's Window. Gently shake your runes in your rune bag and cast them blindly down upon the surface.

The runes you will read are those that fall within the circle in any quadrant and which fell facing right-side up so that you can see the stave. Those that have fallen stave-side down are unexpressed potential. Those that have fallen outside the window are unseen in this situation. Next, look to see which runes in the window have clustered. This represents the heart of the problem. Those that are outliers are only peripheral influences.

Observe which part of the circle the runes fell in. Clusters in the upper half indicate a positive outcome or a favorable reading in general, but if the runes mostly fall in clusters in the lower half, the reading will be full of warnings for you. If runes fall more on the right half of the circle, the problem and its solution are more practical and logical in nature, whereas if they fall more to the left, the problem has a stronger emotional component and requires inner work or social maneuvering.

Order of Interpretation

Step 1: First, find the crux of the situation by either finding the blank rune, if you've chosen to use one, or reading clusters of runes. Clusters of runes should always be interpreted together.

Step 2: Look for any lines leading from the center of the circle outward. These tell a story about the progress of the situation, so you should read them in order from the center to the exterior of Finn's Window. This is a case where you should read runes that are outside the window together with the line as long as they are a clear continuation of the line.

Step 3: Any other runes that fall inside the window should be read next as auxiliary to the situation. The runes that are shown outside the window are not a part of the problem or the situation, but they can be read for reassurance that they are not. For example, if reading on a divorce and a rune that you think represents an ex-wife falls outside the window, you can rest assured that she's not trying to meddle and make the situation worse.

Step 4: Verify for yourself the general solution to the problem by looking if the runes fall in the right- or left-hand sides of the window.

Step 5: Finally, confirm whether the outcome is positive or negative by looking at whether they fall in the upper or lower half of the window. Of course, you'll notice the pattern on these last two steps right away, but it's always good to listen to all the advice of the runes before deciding your fate. You also want to deliver the entire message if you're giving a rune reading to someone else.

Finn's Window is complicated for a beginner to learn, but it gives a firm foundation in several vital rune-reading skills. Therefore, even though it's not the simplest technique, I've introduced it at this stage so that you can learn the skills that Finn's Window reinforces. Then you can use them in other rune-reading methods as well. The fun thing about Finn's Window is that the diagram itself is simple. It can be drawn in the sand. In a pinch, you can even simply visualize the window, and even the object placed in the center, in your mind's eye. All of these devices used for runic divination are just tools, after all. The real runes all exist within you, and as a beginner you're using tools to learn the runes and to integrate them into your life consciously. Runes are not a crutch for your intuition but an extension of your birthright as a human to use language—language creates ideas that then manifest real things in the world.

Some people choose not to use charts or even to cast the runes at all. Laying the runes out gently is one option for rune sets that are delicate, such as those made of desiccated bones or fragile crystal, or those marked with paint, marker, or even blood that easily chips or rubs off from rune casting. Those who wish to lay out runes gently use a tarot card–reading method called "spreads." Tarot cards are decks of cards used since the eighteenth century to tell fortunes by laying the cards out in particular patterns called tarot spreads. The positions of the cards in the spread give context to each card, and this same technique was later applied to runes.

Rune Aspects

Another rune reading-technique, borrowed from astrology, is the practice of reading runes by the angle or "aspect" at which they lie in relationship to one another in a rune spread or diagram. The best way for a beginner to understand aspects is with the simple spread diagram below. This spread can be used for any topic of focus or question.

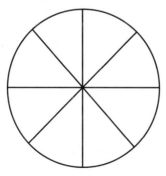

Aspect Diagram

An aspect diagram looks just like a pie chart with eight sections. To use this chart, cast the runes and let them rest where they may. For learning purposes, the first time that you use this chart you might wish to arrange the runes within the slices that they seem to be falling into if they land partially on a line. You might also wish to rotate all of the runes by hand so that the top of each rune is at the outside of the circle and the bottom of each rune is at the tip of the section.

The runes that fall directly across from one another affect each other negatively. Runes that are at a 90-degree angle from one another in the diagram also cause some opposition or try to block each other's energies in your life. However, the runes that are at a 45-degree angle from one another, or less, positively affect one another. Some advanced runemasters read aspects of runes in all runecasts by observing the angle that each rune takes in relationship to every other rune. You don't have to read rune aspects in every reading, but experimenting with this chart can help you grow as a beginner by showing how even generally negative runes can affect other runes positively and vice versa. For example, hagalaz can be softened with the presence of ingwaz in a relationship reading, since certainly any new beginning in a sexual relationship can be frenetic and awkward. However, hagalaz can make uruz into a negative situation in a reading on a potential wedding date, emphasizing a strong storm passing through.

Rune Pulling

Before we dive into rune spreads, let's take a look at the practice of merely pulling a rune from your bag. This is sometimes called "drawing a rune" or a "one-rune spread." Pulling a rune a day is a wonderful way to familiarize yourself with the runes and to memorize them, especially if you take the time to meditate upon the rune as well. Here's a rune-pulling practice that you can start tomorrow.

Rune-Pulling Practice

Step 1: Keep a bag of runes at your bedside along with your rune journal and a writing implement. If you're on autopilot in the morning, place your bag on top of something you know you'll reach for, like your glasses, watch, or morning vitamins or medications. Upon rising in the morning, pull a rune at random from the bag, closing your hand around the first rune that you touch or feeling for the spiritual energy of the right rune. Spiritual energy might feel like buzzing, fuzziness, warmth, pressure, or something else. Different people sense energy in different ways, and that's okay. After you choose your rune, look at the stave even if you are looking at the back side of the rune when you first open your hand. It's okay to turn a rune over when rune pulling. Copy the stave into your rune journal and jot down any initial ideas about what the rune might mean about your day. For example, if you drew the rune hagalaz, it's a clear warning. Think about your day and what might prompt such a warning. If you're gearing up for a road trip, it might mean needing to be extra careful on the road and to check your oil and tires to make sure you won't have a blowout. If the weather outside looks threatening, hagalaz might literally portend hail.

Step 2: Go about your day but be mindful about the rune that you pulled in the morning. If you see the rune's influence come to pass, write about it immediately. This expression of the rune you pulled can now be added as an interpretation in your rune journal. Whenever it comes up in the future, you'll have a very concrete example of what it might mean for you.

Step 3: When it is time for bed, take a moment to transfer any of your notes that you made throughout the day into your rune journal. If you did not see the rune's influence come to pass, it's okay to write about this too. This is a learning process, after all. Take some time to meditate while gazing upon the rune before sleep. It is okay if you fall asleep looking at the rune. In fact, I was taught as a child that if I fell asleep thinking about something, I would commit it to memory. This old folk wisdom has served me well.

I've laid out rune pulling as a discipline that will help you become a strong runewita with a lifelong tie to the runes. However, the process can be pared down to take a mere moment of your time if you'd like to integrate runes into your life in a simpler way. The key is to make your runes accessible. Keep them at your computer desk in plain sight or even in your car. You'll have something to occupy your time while taking a break or waiting in a parking lot for someone. Don't check your runes at stoplights, of course, or when driving. I'm pretty sure that divination while driving is just as bad as texting while driving. Let handling the runes be a welcome break in your day. Take a deep breath and pull a rune from the bag whenever you like. Gaze upon it and return it to the bag knowing that you've enriched your spirituality just a little bit by this simple and ancient practice.

Rune Spreads

Now let's explore the practice of rune spreads. These can range from the incredibly simple to the complex. Rune spreads can use a single rune or every rune in the bag. Some advanced spreads even combine rune sets. I'll teach you the basics here, and then you can look at some more example spreads in chapter 3 for each topic that interests you. Rune spreads are an important practice for the beginner to learn for two reasons: First, using spreads makes interpretation simpler because the meaning ascribed to the position in the spread can narrow down your options when there's more than one interpretation possible for that rune. Second, since spreads are used for tarot cards as well, knowing the rune spreads provides a skill that you can use to branch out into other forms of divination. As a result, you become a stronger divination practitioner.

A spread does not require a special marked surface, although some people do choose to make elaborate cloths onto which the spreads are diagrammed. A spread can be committed to memory or used while looking at the diagram on an unmarked table.

Without further ado, let's get started on the best beginner multiple-rune spreads.

Three Rune Spread

The three-rune spread is the best beginner rune spread because it can be applied to any topic, and it also makes readings much more clear. For the three-rune spread, you will pull three runes and lay them out in one line. Flip over any runes that are overturned. For spreads, it's okay to interpret all the runes you see because you're pulling only a specific number. The unexpressed runes remain in your bag the whole time.

The first rune represents the past, the second rune represents the present, and the third rune represents the future. This can make rune readings much clearer because if you draw wunjo, for example, you don't have to wonder whether the rune refers to a blessing that has already happened or is just about to happen. The spread does some of the interpretation work for you.

Try out the three-rune spread for several different questions or topics. A three-rune spread on your love life will be interpreted differently from a three-rune spread on your financial situation. Spreads help show you the runes' versatility while also giving your interpretations more precision. You'll still have to use some intuitive sense when choosing between two different possible meanings for a rune, but spreads give you a framework within which you can work.

Thor's Hammer

Thor's Hammer is a very common spread that you can use when you feel you're ready to move on to a slightly larger spread. It can also be used for many topics. Though it's simple enough for a beginner, I know many professional rune readers who use this spread almost exclusively when reading runes for their clients. The spread is named with a nod toward Thor, an ancient Norse god of thunder who wields a hammer, since ancient Norse people used runes, and the layout of the spread is supposed to look a little something like a hammer. In the diagram below, the numbers represent the order in which the runes are laid out in their positions, as well as the order in which the runes are read.

3

2   5   4

1

1. Influences
2. Warnings
3. Blessings
4. Outcome
5. Long-term destiny

Choose a topic for your reading and try to figure out a problem using Thor's Hammer. It can be nice to get some divine wisdom and to look at your situation from an outside perspective. This spread also offers the chance to see both warnings and blessings. You're always going to get to see the silver lining, so this is a great spread to do for a situation that has you feeling down in the dumps. It's interesting how sometimes a "bad" rune will be placed into the blessing position. This is one way that the power of runes can let you see some of your weaknesses as strengths.

Reversals

In ancient times, people wrote runes upside down and even flipped backward at random. It could have been that the way the rune was facing was simply not important to the original runemasters. However, in divination, reading runes differently when they are cast upside down, or if you see them upside down when you lay them down blindly in a spread, is another technique that has been imported from tarot-card reading. Such runes are called "reversals" and they are most often read as an extreme and negative version of the upright rune. Many runes cannot be reversals because they look the same upside down and right-side up. I think I can make a strong case that beginners should not read reversals. Not only is it historically inaccurate to read them this way (and many of us do want to keep true to the old ways), but reading rune reversals adds a lot of negativity and needless complexity to a rune reading. However, I include this mention of reversals just in case you feel like you are ready for the technique of reversals and want to hear all the bad news and warnings you can possibly hear. Hey, there's something to be said about being prepared for the worst that can happen.

Weaving a Meaningful Story with Runes

The hardest part about any form of divination is weaving a coherent answer out of what you see in front of your face. As a beginner, you'll be looking back and forth between your runecast or spread and the book to interpret them. This might make you feel as if you're just reading out words at random, each one having nothing to do with the other. Take heart that an initial feeling of confusion about how interpretations fit is normal. The trick is to tune in to your intuition instead of your common sense, and that takes time to learn. It takes even more time to gain comfort with the practice. A rune reading is not like a crossword puzzle—it's more like a Choose Your Own Adventure book that is still being written.

The runes contain all of the potential of the human experience. Some people point out that the runes can fit into every phase of the hero's journey. This is the archetypical story identified by mythologist Joseph Campbell that gets told over and over again in every major myth from *The Odyssey* to *Star Wars*. I like to tell people who are new to experiencing a rune reading that when cast at random or laid out in spreads, the runes can tell a whole story.

Every story has a beginning, a middle, and an end. The beginning of the reading should start with a description of the past or the situation as it is shown by the runes. The middle of a rune reading should be spent looking for the protagonists and any "bad guys" or big cliffhangers and climaxes. You don't have to tell the end of anyone's story, but the end of a reading typically comes with a look at the future, an outcome, or an overview.

The best way for a beginner to become proficient at the process of creating fluid readings is to gradually wean off reading rune interpretations from the book. Go back to the first chapter of this book under the subheading "The Elder Futhark Runes" and also make sure that you've created and are writing in your rune journal if you're struggling to remember and construct rune meanings. With daily practice, you can learn this skill and keep it for life. After you've memorized the meanings and have started the lifelong process of adding personalized meanings of your own, start practicing the three-rune spread to tell short stories with your runes. If you're already proficient at doing a daily one-rune reading or pulling a rune for yourself, try graduating up to doing a three-rune reading for yourself or someone else every day.

Since there are so many magical scripts and so many related divination techniques, they sometimes blend together with the runes. This is because we're all still learning how best to use them. The ancients did not pass down to us a complete guide as to how they used the runes. Many contemporaries have filled in the gaps in our knowledge with rich sources of information from astrology, palmistry, and other arts. Our insights improve the art, while bringing rune casting closer to its roots. Perhaps you will be the next great runemaster to make a meaningful breakthrough with the runes.

Divination with the Ogham

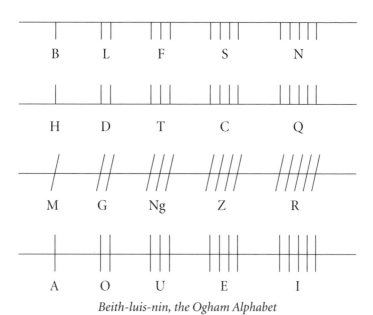

Beith-luis-nin, the Ogham Alphabet

The ogham is often confused for runes by beginners because both are ancient scripts that were used for divination and both are still used for magic, writing, and divination today. In fact, Finn's Window is borrowed from ancient lore about ogham, not runes. Much like futhark comes from the six initial letters of its alphabet, the ogham is called the *Beith-luis-nin* after the first letters in its script. One aspect of ogham that can be adapted to runes is the tradition of marking them on sticks for divination, rather than on stones or small rounds of wood. The sticks can be cast onto Finn's Window just like runes, or they can be drawn at random, sort of like drawing straws. I mention this form of divination because it can be used with any runic system and is an easily crafted alternative for those who want to carve runes into wood but don't have access to a saw to slice a big branch into rounds. Simply gather enough sticks for all of your runes and carve the runes into each stick. Paint or even a ballpoint pen will do in a pinch. The sticks can be placed in a decorative vase to be drawn at random whenever you wish to consult the runes. Using the ogham method of divination with runes can be a discreet and beautiful way to incorporate runes into your life.

Horoscope Rune Spread

By far the simplest way to introduce yourself to astrology through rune readings is to use the runes as a tool to explore your horoscope for the year ahead. Simply pull twelve runes at random and lay them face-up before you in a circle. Place a thirteenth rune in the center of the circle. Starting at the top, read the circle for the months ahead. So, if it is presently January, the topmost rune would represent January, and the and the one to its right would represent February. The rune in the center represents your theme for the year, which ties them all together. I use this spread frequently with clients, as it can be very helpful for timing questions. For example, you might ask, "What month is a good month for taking the next step in my career?" You can assess each of the runes for what they mean regarding your work life. Not only will some months stand out immediately as more positive than others, but you'll also get specific advice from the runes as to what steps you should take to move your career ahead and when to do so.

Once you've mastered this basic horoscope spread, try out the following personality spread, which incorporates a little more from the realms of astrology.

Astrology Personality Spread

Lay twelve runes in a circle with their faces upright, pulling them at random from your bag. These represent the twelve astrological houses, which in Western astrology are usually calculated with birth time and location. I love to reach for this personality analysis as an option if my client doesn't know his or her birth time or is asking for a reading on somebody whose birthdate is unknown. In particular, expectant mothers love this spread to get a possible peek at the personality of their unborn children. Here are the houses and their meanings so that you can do a chart of one's personality and life with the runes:

1. Your personality characteristics, traits, and quirks

2. Your view toward money and material things

3. Your childhood and views toward study and travel

4. Your family and your cultural, national, and ancestral roots

5. Love, creativity, children, hobbies, sports, and games

6. Work, health, pets, and other duties

7. Close and deep relationships, including business relationships and friendships

8. Your views toward sex, death, spirituality, and commitment

9. Spirituality and journeys, both literal and figurative

10. Your social status, independent pursuits, and ambitions

11. Friendships, collaborations, acquaintances, associates, groups, and alliances in your life

12. Your inspirations and spiritual mysteries that are for you to solve

This personality profile can be very complete. However, sometimes you'll just want to get a snapshot of a personality in the reading. For example, my clients often ask, "What will my next significant other be like?" This is a rather open-ended question, and the runes can show many different answers describing the personality of the unknown person. Adding some astrological correspondences can be helpful. If you do a one-rune draw and pull fehu, for example, the rune is telling you that your next significant other will be an Aries. This can tell you a lot about the person's personality as well as give you a hint as to his or her birthday. I've known clients who wanted to know a potential love's sign ahead of time in order to filter online dating profiles.

three

Love, Money, and Career and School Readings

Fortune-telling is the best job in the world. I get up in the morning and help clients with all sorts of questions in my office or around the world through the Internet. Nothing surprises me anymore. I've been asked every question under the sun. With my experience, I know that most people come to a fortune-teller with a pressing question or at least a situation on their minds, unless they're just trying one out for fun at a party or a festival. So I have a feeling that you might be more likely to reach for your runes if there's something weighing on your mind. Relying on runes for spiritual guidance is not a bad thing. Runes are a tool for your own intuition as well as a sacred connection to the divine. The use of runes for divination can be thought of as a form of prayer or meditation, a devotion just as useful as any other spiritual duty or practice. I've drawn from my own years of experience to give you a collection of the most common topics that people bring to the runes or any other divinatory tool, for that matter. This chapter includes some practical ways to address them and a plan for attacking your problem with the runes as a powerful spiritual tool.

When using the runes for divination on a specific important topic, a new pressure and anxiety can build upon the reader that might not otherwise be there if you're just practicing with general readings. You may ask yourself which of the methods you've already learned is the most accurate and which tells you the most detailed information from your runes. It's important to know the difference between precision and accuracy. Accuracy means that the information is consistently spot on. Precision means that the information is very detailed and not too general. Ideally, you want your readings to be both accurate and precise. Reading on specific topics can increase the precision of your readings, but only practice and experience (as well as a bit of luck and help from the gods) can increase your accuracy as a reader. It's easy for beginners to become overwhelmed by the variation in rune techniques. I understand completely, because this is a natural part of the process of learning a new skill that involves intuition.

When I learned karate, I began by practicing drills of how to punch, block, and kick. But the first time that I went to spar with an opponent, I didn't know what to do or which one of my limbs to move first. It took me years of practice before I could intuitively respond to the lay of the land and to the problem in front of me. Likewise, the awkward feeling of not being sure whether you're choosing the right answers in a rune reading is perfectly normal. I experienced this same learning curve when I first started learning to dance as an adult. I learned a few moves but still didn't know which ones to bust out when the music came on. Now that you've learned some rune reading methods, the runes are your dance or sparring partners. You'll have to anticipate what you need them to do and then go with the flow and your own intuition.

This chapter offers some concrete examples of how to get the answers you need about the topics that hold your heart. I've organized each topic into four sections. First, I'll lay out some expectations about what the runes can and cannot say about the subject at hand. Next, I'll give some examples of rune-casting charts that can be used to discover information you might want. Then, I'll give you some rune-pulling spreads, which is another way to give the proper context to the runes. Finally, I'll show you how the runes themselves can be interpreted to fit the topic with greater precision.

Love

One of my recent clients came to me for help with love and requested that I use the runes because he felt an ancestral connection with them. He wanted to know whether it was the right time for him to marry. He explained that he was already currently dating a nice girl but wasn't sure if he was ready for marriage in general. He had always wanted to grow up, get married, and have children. To complicate matters, his parents, who lived on another continent, had started nagging him that he was starting to get too old to marry and have children. His mom wanted him to travel home on his holiday vacation to meet another girl she had picked out for him and thought would be an excellent marriage match. His mother and father disapproved of him contemplating marriage with a woman in the United States and hoped he would consider marrying within his own nationality and ethnicity. He wanted to know which girl would be best for him in the long run for marriage and family.

Overall, the runes indicated, to his surprise and relief, that either woman could lead to marriage and family. However, since it was his own inner desire that caused him to date his current girlfriend, the runes indicated it would be a more emotionally joyful path, initially, if he popped the question to her. However, the runes also advised that he would never feel completely ready to take the plunge into marriage and would need to push past his anxiety.

The reading made sense to my client, and he remarked about how he hadn't ever felt ready to leave home and move so far away to a country where he didn't speak the language. I remember telling my client about how I hadn't felt ready to be a parent until I gazed at the face of my first-born child; I wasn't ready until it happened to me. We mused about how deep and philosophical the runes can sometimes be, causing us to look beyond a love problem to consider the nature of love itself.

The most popular topic among clients who come to me to have their fortunes told is the future of their love lives. As a happily married woman celebrating the tenth anniversary of her blessed handfasting this year, I still need a little divine help with being a kinder wife. Many of my clients ask me about old flames or new crushes, wondering how another person is feeling or what to do next in order to take some chemistry with a crush to the next level. I've used runes to help set lucky wedding dates and to give the go-ahead to couples moving in together or simply going out for a second date. I've even seen the runes announce the potential for pregnancy, which can be either cause for celebration or a warning to use protection if a pregnancy would be ill timed. The runes can definitely help one's love life enormously when used in the proper way. However, with any divination tool, it's important to avoid getting stuck endlessly analyzing the topic.

Expectations

When clients come to me as a fortune-teller, they often have some unreasonable expectations about what can be predicted. They want to know the name of their soul mate, the day and time they will meet, what he or she will look like, and where they will first cross paths. I can relate to the desire to be in control and in full knowledge of one's own life. I like to be at the steering wheel of my own destiny, and it can be frustrating to be forced to wait and learn and grow as a person. I could tell you some stories about how I raged at my spiritual teachers, practically demanding to be elevated through the ranks as a priestess simply because I felt I had paid my dues and spent my time in the student's seat, so to speak. But in the real world, the future is written in sand instead of stone. We make choices in every moment that send ripple effects out into our destinies. So even if you threw some runes in a love reading and they all turned out very positive for marriage, you could choose to take a vow of celibacy tomorrow and turn away from that destiny entirely.

Therefore, it's important to set clear expectations for what you want from the runes, and in order to do that you'll need to think first about what you will do with the information. So many times a client has come to me asking about an ex-boyfriend or ex-girlfriend, hoping that a lost love will return. Even if the runes all point to the fact that the past love has moved on and will not return, the client still chooses to pursue the ex-lover. I don't judge the choice to keep hope alive, but there is no point to asking whether or not a lover will return if the answer will not affect your actions. Before you touch those runes, be sure that you are willing to act on their advice. If not, that means that you need to change your question before you begin.

The runes are pictograms, so they will not tell you what a potential spouse will look like, unless you already have preexisting clairvoyant talent. It is unlikely that the runes will tell you a name. In my extensive experience, when Elder Futhark runes are sounded out in a reading, they more often than not will give a nonsense word. Retrospectively, some clients have told me that the nonsense word turned out to be a name that was abbreviated and blended together, as the ancients often wrote runes without spaces and made short cuts whenever possible. However, for that you'd need to have some serious riddle-solving prowess, and I think that name reading is an unreasonable expectation for a beginner. Casting two runes hoping to see initials is a simpler way to divine a name, but I ask that you realistically decide how you would use the information of initials of a potential lover. If you're not going to pore through the phone book and call everyone with those initials or reject any dates from people without those initials, you're probably wasting your time. I encourage you to think of practical ways to use your runes' answers instead of asking the runes to paint you into a corner.

Savvy clients of mine ask questions that empower them to find or keep love. Here are some sample questions that make me raise my eyebrows and know that these rune fans mean business:

- What should I be thinking about as I browse dating profiles online in order to pick whom to contact?
- How can I heal from my past relationship so that I am ready to welcome new love into my life?
- I want my marriage to be more stable. What can I do in order to increase the likelihood of a positive outcome for my relationship's rocky situation?
- What are the strengths and weaknesses of the potential pairing of myself and my crush as a couple?
- How will I know when I'm ready to ask my girlfriend to marry me?
- Should I get married and have a family or pursue academics and a career at this stage of my life?
- What are the personality characteristics of a good love match for me?
- How should I react to what my boyfriend said last night?
- What should I be aware of in order to ensure the best outcome of my divorce for all concerned, including my children?

Charts

Recall that rune charts are diagrams onto which you will randomly cast your runes. To try out a new chart, I like to roughly draw the chart on a large piece of paper. A flattened box and a thick marker can be the makings of a great practice rune chart. Or, if it's dry enough, you can draw simple charts in dirt or sand. If you find the rune chart useful, you can then construct a more permanent option out of cloth and keep it folded with your rune bag if you choose.

Compatibility Chart

My husband and I are pretty compatible people. We are both passionate and excited about our goals. We both can be fairly spontaneous. We both love to learn about new things, and to gather people together at our home. Plenty of things about us are incompatible as well. We certainly don't have compatible politics! That doesn't mean that we aren't a smart match. In fact, incompatibility can be a great life teacher, encouraging selflessness and empathy. Some give and take of learning to cohabitate is necessary when a couple has some incompatibilities. Don't let compatibility be an insurmountable barrier to exploring a relationship. However, compatibility readings can help you realize your strengths and weaknesses as a couple or potential couple. It helps to know what you're up against if you're in for a relationship that will be a bit of a battle. If you choose to proceed, it's important to stop and re-evaluate your relationship at various points on your journey, asking yourself if he or she is worth it.

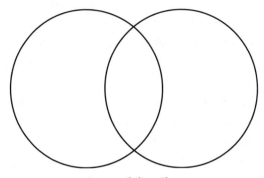

Compatibility Chart

If you need a refresher on how to perform a chart reading, hop back to chapter 2 and reread the "Rune Charts" section. Essentially, the compatibility chart is a large Venn diagram, showing you which characteristics are compatible and which are incompatible, with the overlapping middle section showcasing your strengths as a couple. It is best to read the incompatibilities as advice. Think about the meaning of the rune shown for each person and consider how this powerful trait can be made into a blessing in your relationship. I've always done compatibility chart readings with the female on the left and the man on the right for heterosexual relationships. For same-sex relationships I allow the client to choose at random, and we hold that designation in our minds. Sometimes I even add additional circles to the diagram if reading for families with children or other larger groups of people in a relationship together.

Essentially, this diagram allows for runes that would otherwise be worrying in a compatibility reading to appear as strengths in this context. For example, if I were doing a compatibility reading for a client without the chart, thurisaz would not be a good sign. I'd let the client know that her potential boyfriend would be like a thorn in her side, perhaps by constantly implying that she wasn't good enough. However, if I were using the chart and thurisaz landed in the middle of the two circles, it would become the strength of a couple. Perhaps one would fiercely defend and protect the other through a battle with cancer, or maybe sharp wit and banter are the core of this relationship. As with many things in life, challenges can become blessings.

Testing the Waters Chart:
Discover the Thoughts and Feelings of Another

Some divination practitioners frown upon the idea of reading on the topic of another person without his or her consent; third-party readings can be viewed as invasive. I choose to perform third-party readings because I believe that it's natural to try to gauge another person's motivations with my intuition. The energies in the universe are free to be read using runes, just as the air on our planet is free to breathe and share. It is impossible to entirely reign in one's intuition for ethical reasons and is not necessary since the reader won't be directly changing that other person's energy without his or her permission. This chart is helpful when trying to understand how you affect another person. When a client asks me "How did my boyfriend react emotionally to that e-mail I sent him?" I reach for this chart.

Testing the Waters Chart

The imagery of the Testing the Waters Chart is a heart with an arrow through it, a traditional symbol of love. The arrow spans the reading surface area. Runes that land nearer to the point of the arrow represent the future, while those that land on or near the fletching at the tail end represent the past. Runes that land within the heart represent emotional feelings—potentially of love, depending upon the rune in context. Runes landing above the heart tend more toward platonic or even spiritual feelings. Runes landing below the heart represent base needs that could be sexual, financial, or otherwise material.

If the client wants to ask how this person thinks and feels about another person, a symbol or object from the other person can be placed elsewhere on the chart. For example, I gave two sisters a reading at a bachelorette party. One of the sisters asked about her crush, and the two bickered good-naturedly about how he might actually prefer the other sister. I set up to do the reading for the person with the crush but asked to have an object from her sister to include in the reading. Her sister handed me her sunglasses, and I placed them above and away from the heart. After I allowed the first sister to cast the runes for us, far more runes indicating positive and romantic intentions fell near her sister's sunglasses, proving his heart's true desire to us.

Spreads

If you need a reminder about how to perform a rune reading that involves a spread, head back to "Rune Spreads" in chapter 2 to jog your memory.

Spread to Choose between Two Lovers or Potential Lovers

Sometimes compatibility isn't an issue for a client who has an abundance of lovers but chooses, or is forced by circumstances to choose, only one. A seven-rune spread can be done quickly to discover which lover is a better fit for a person. Think of this spread as exploring two different potential destinies. Hopefully, one of the potential paths will demonstrate a clear winner. As with the Venn diagram–style chart, you'll have to designate which lover is which in the reading. The position of one lover or another in the spread is an arbitrary decision, but do hold your choices in your mind for a moment before you lay out your runes.

$$3 \qquad 6$$
$$2 \quad 7 \quad 5$$
$$1 \qquad 4$$

Each lover has a lower rune that represents the past foundation on which the future can be built, a middle rune that represents the present situation, and then an upper rune that represents the future if you traveled along the path of a relationship with that person. The rune in the center of the two columns contains special advice or any further information you need to know before choosing one of these two lovers. In some cases, a rather negative rune will show up as the center rune, indicating that neither of these lovers is a good option and you'd do best to try to find a different person entirely.

In this spread, the story that is told of the journey through these potential relationships is more important than the overall goodness or badness of the runes. For example, imagine that one lover showed hagalaz followed by neid and then jera. The other lover sports wunjo followed by isa and then dagaz. The additional rune in between the two is raido. At first glance, the presence of hagalaz might cause one to reject the first lover, and the presence of wunjo might favor the second. However, notice how the journey changes along each potential relationship. Though the first potential relationship seems to start off at a rocky patch in life, the two needing the support of one another seems to result in a happy ending to the journey. The second potential relationship, however, starts out happy but then grinds to a halt with isa. Though dagaz can mean beginnings as well as endings, I wouldn't be optimistic following isa. The addition of raido seems to highlight the importance of progress in a relationship, so the lover that promotes the most progress is the clear winner here.

The "I Can't Forget My Ex!" Spread

I had to include a good spread about obsessing over an ex because I deal with so many clients who are still heartbroken about an ex from months or even years past. A very good friend of mine still struggles with emotional issues over an ex who simply disappeared into thin air without even leaving a note. It doesn't take a psychic to know that in the vast majority of cases of one person pining over an ex, there's very little chance of a reunion. Life must press on, one way or another, and the runes can help confirm whether one should hold out some small hope for rekindling romance or throw oneself wholeheartedly into the painful process of addressing emotional regrets.

3   4

2

1

    The "I Can't Forget My Ex!" Spread is shaped like a Y. The rune at the bottom indicates why you are having a problem moving forward from the relationship. A positive rune may indicate a proper chance of having at least a platonic relationship with the ex in the present time, while a negative rune may indicate a personal emotional issue that requires healing. At the crux of the Y is a rune that shows you the present situation with your ex. The left-hand arm of the Y shows you what would be a necessary outcome in your life if you decided to continue to pursue the ex. I include this option because many clients come to me with minds already made up to give undying love to an ex, regardless of whether that love will remain unrequited. Depending on the rune that is laid here, the message may be to reduce communication, establish a platonic friendship, make a friends-with-benefits arrangement, or even facilitate a true romantic reunion. The right-hand arm of the Y shows the potential outcome of moving on from the ex.

The spread may confirm that moving on is possible, even though it may seem difficult at this moment. Even a challenging rune may show the necessary steps to achieving freedom from memories and hopes for a love lost. If something like ken shows up, you may be able to rekindle a passion, and ingwaz can indicate the potential for a friends-with-benefits arrangement. The presence of the rune isa may be a bummer because you know that things cannot move forward with that ex, but it doesn't necessarily mean that things can't move on for yourself. Look at surrounding runes for guidance when things aren't going the way you hoped. Dagaz may show a new door opening as soon as you find closure on this relationship, which means that you can find someone new.

Rune Meanings in Context

Once you have memorized the rune meanings you need and have become acquainted with how they play out in your life, you can apply them to matters of the heart for more specific advice. The process of learning new twists and perspectives on runes can take time. I'd like to give you some examples of how I often see rune meanings shift and change as they are applied to love readings. These are just my own examples from personal experience, so yours might evolve differently—and that's okay. Now is the time to pull out your rune journal, and as you read for your own love life, you can log the specific love meanings of the runes as they become apparent to you.

Fehu: This signifies a relationship that will take time and care to develop but could become a reliable resource. There is something of deep value here. Sacrifices may be necessary, but such sacrifices are well worth it. A successful relationship is built upon effort from both parties. The potential for having children is here.

Uruz: Tremendous passion is at work here, but there is no plan or direction. Progress may appear to come in short bursts but without serious thought as to what the future might look like in the relationship, so as a result it may be impossible to take things to the next level. You can't force another person to feel a certain way.

Thurisaz: A person is nagging or negative. There may be an external influence souring a relationship, such as a meddling ex or a flirtatious new person drawing energy and attention away. Harsh words cannot be forgotten, and they may be the undoing of the relationship because of spite. There is a wedge between people in the relationship, so this rune can indicate the path to a breakup.

Ansuz: Listen to advice about this relationship from friends or family because the advice is good advice. This can be hard to hear if other people do not approve of the object of your affections, but sometimes others know you best or can provide proper outside perspective. Communication is needed when this rune shows up, so see it as encouragement to get everything out on the table. Share your true feelings.

Raido: Love may be found during travel. There may be a long-distance relationship indicated. Forward motion is always implied, which means if you can't progress now, then it is time to move right along to another lover. Negative cycles may keep repeating themselves, developing resentment or fear. I sometimes see this rune show up when one person in a relationship is happy with the way things are while the other wants things to progress.

Ken: A new passion is alighting. A new beginning must occur. This rune is a good sign if you're not in a relationship but are searching for one. However, this rune can be a bad sign if you are currently in a relationship. It means that your passions are allowing a boil to fester in the relationship. If you don't work to create a new beginning in your current relationship, one or both of you will sabotage its future in order to force one.

Gebo: A proposal is imminent! Generosity is the foundation upon which a relationship can be built. Stepping out of your comfort zone and giving until it hurts may be necessary to strengthen your partnership. A new relationship or new arrangements in a current relationship may be forming. You may be moving in together if you haven't already.

Wunjo: Pleasure is to be found in this relationship. He or she definitely likes you in return. Any risks taken will be well rewarded when this rune appears. If you've yet to tell her that you love her or to swoop in for that first kiss, it is time to go for it. If there is an argument of any kind going on, you will soon be the winner.

Hagalaz: A breakup or shake-up is imminent. The relationship as it is cannot possibly survive. You must demolish the present relationship in order to move onward. The only way that this rune can show up with the couple remaining together is to make drastic change, which could involve taking a break and rebuilding a new version of the relationship from the ground up.

Neid: There is sexual chemistry here. In a relationship reading, one person may be relying too much on the other person, leaving a feeling of suffocation. The relationship may be codependent in some way. Be warned that a person who seems to be attracted to you may just be using you for material gain or social status.

Isa: No progress is possible. If you're crushing on someone, it's a no-go. Perhaps he already has a girlfriend, or perhaps she's not even interested in someone of your gender. If this reading is done on an ex, it means the relationship is definitely over for good. If this rune is drawn on a current relationship, the status quo will be maintained. If you're hoping to take this relationship to the next level, it will be impossible.

Jera: There is long-term potential here. When the reading is done on a blossoming relationship, know that at first progress will seem very slow, but things will get rolling and last for the long haul. When done on a current relationship, jera can indicate a new and beautiful evolution. Lovers may be moving in with one another for the first time or retiring and moving to a new home together. A couple may begin a hobby or business that will bring joy and positive change as well as possibly money.

Eihwaz: An ultimatum is at hand. This rune can give permission to give an ultimatum to a partner, such as asking to get married or else break up. This ultimatum will likely be rewarded, as the rune suggests that the relationship can endure trials. If this rune comes up in a potential relationship, it encourages calculated risks. It's okay to ask him out, as he is likely to say yes.

Pertho: Risky sexual behavior is happening. Make sure to wear protection if you're engaging in a sexual relationship with somebody. This rune isn't always bad news, though. If you're a flirtatious type and want to try to make a move on somebody, now is your time. Live for the moment and go with the flow.

Algiz: A friendship is at the base of a relationship. The good news is that the relationship potential here is stable and lasting. The bad news is that this is a cool, calm, and platonic rune rather than a passionate one. If you pull this rune when gauging a crush's interest in you, it may show that he only likes you as a friend.

Sowilo: Joy and success are coming your way in love. Emotions will be high at a wedding or special date. Communications may burst through and bring things to light that were once hidden from view. When this rune appears, it is a "go ahead" symbol for what you're planning. Tell her you love her. Propose marriage. Keep your eye out for a shining light to enter your life if you're not yet in a relationship.

Tiwaz: This can represent a man entering someone's love life. When this rune appears, it means that decisive action is necessary. You'll have to take the lead and make the first move, otherwise nothing will happen. In a relationship reading, this indicates a need for fairness. It can't always be one person compromising or putting all the effort into the relationship. If you can't make progress through your own force of will, consider striking out on your own and taking some time as a single person.

Berkanan: Pregnancy and children could be in your future. This rune can also represent a woman when it appears in a reading. Thus, this rune can be lucky news for somebody hoping to have kids or for somebody looking for a woman to love.

Ehwaz: The good news is that this rune represents loyalty. However, this is a rather cool and platonic rune, rather than a passionate one. So, if this is pulled for a love potential, it may mean that he or she thinks of you as family rather than as a love interest. In a relationship reading, this rune can be a positive component of a healthy relationship.

Mannaz: Two people are on the same wavelength. Communicate well to act as a team together. If there is a love problem, taking a look at it from another perspective and puzzling it out intellectually can help. This rune can sometimes indicate that other people outside the relationship may be affecting it, either positively or negatively depending on any surrounding runes.

Laguz: This is a rune of love, so it is a very auspicious sign in a love reading. This represents deep feelings of romantic love that are worthy of a strong relationship. The advice of this rune is to go within yourself to assess your true feelings and to learn how to express them to others in order to make your relationship better or to draw love to you.

Ingwaz: This is a sexual rune. Sex is in the making. There will be a first time, whether it be a first kiss or a new sort of relationship that has never been had before. Prepare for exciting change to the status quo. Be careful about getting carried away, because once you cross this bridge there might be no coming back.

Othila: In love readings, this rune represents your home space. If you live with the object of your affection, the advice is to focus on making your home life more peaceful. If you are not yet in a relationship, this rune suggests that spring cleaning at home may draw love to you by making it a more welcoming place. Pay attention to your dreams, especially if they have advice from ancestors about your love life.

Dagaz: Every beginning must have its end. This rune indicates that an imbalance cannot last for long, and resolution is imminent. A mutual breakup may be the outcome. For somebody who is not in a relationship, this rune suggests that you must leave behind baggage from a past relationship in order to begin a new one.

The Blank Rune: There is nothing that you can personally do to make your relationship better or your love life worse. It's time to take time for yourself, whether it means learning to love the single life or simply taking a break from a significant other to go on a personal retreat.

Money

Yes, I've used the runes to answer my own questions about money, but that doesn't mean that I gamble all of my money on the track betting that the runes have the right answers every time. Instead, the runes often give me some things to think about when making my own choices. I like to think that I usually make good choices about money. A money question I recently asked the runes when I was trying to decide how to best put aside some savings comes to mind.

Last year, I fretted a little bit about whether to make the maximum annual contribution to my retirement account. My husband and I are not anywhere near retirement age, and last year was a rough year for medical bills. I wanted to contribute my normal amount of savings to my retirement nest egg, but I also worried that another medical problem might crop up and I'd need that money applied instead to our health budget. As I cast the runes, I had all sorts of scenarios swirling in my head about misfortunes that might require a large amount of liquid assets.

It would have been nice if the runes had told me, "Hey, no major medical bills hitting next year. Feel free to spend or invest that money as you see fit." Unfortunately, the runes offered me no such assurances. What eihwaz did advise me was to look at the long-term picture of my life, and shut down anything that turns my attention from the road ahead. Under the present circumstances, I decided that meant that I should invest my money in my retirement. After all, there are no perfect circumstances that might cause me to say that I don't need a large portion of my money. It's never fun to store money where it can't be immediately accessed. Instead, I had to have the discipline to put away money even when the future is unknown. It's quite possible that I may have applied my interpretation differently if I had done this rune reading at an earlier stage of my life. Looking at the long-term might have meant paying off student loans when I had them.

If I have the same rune reading thirty years in the future, it might mean leaving money for my grandchildren. Interpretation of the runes is as much about evaluating your beliefs and choices as it is about getting quick answers.

The second most popular topic among clients of my fortune-telling business is money. Often clients don't even care where the money comes from as long as it rolls in and takes care of what is needed. It doesn't matter if the money is from winning the lottery or from years of hard work if it comes in quantity enough to solve problems. An open-minded perspective about money is actually a good thing for divination. It means that you aren't limiting your reading to the one path that you see before you, so you are allowing the runes to guide you in a way that might be unexpected. The true power of the runes is not in telling you what you want to hear but in their ability to give you the advice you need to hear.

Expectations

If I had a nickel for every time a client asked me to predict the numbers to the lottery or to otherwise give specific instructions on how to make a lot of money fast, I'd be well on my way toward a fine sum of money myself. The runes are a spiritual tool, not a replacement for a qualified financial planner. If you truly are in dire need of money to provide yourself with food, shelter, or medical care, it's important to reach for resources other than your runes first. Once you've stabilized your life, you can focus on your spiritual pursuits with more devotion.

That said, there are plenty of money-reading questions in life that are perfectly acceptable for rune consultation. We make so many choices on a daily basis for our work lives, our spending, or other transactions. When picking between two equally great job opportunities or trying to figure out whether it's the right time to retire or buy a house, runes can give food for thought. I'll give you a few example rune charts and spreads, but first I'll show you how to format a good money question for the runes. If you're thinking of money in relation to jobs and careers, those questions will come in the next section, "Career and School."

- What should I be thinking about in order to bring more financial and material security to my life?
- How will I be able to afford my kid's college tuition?
- Am I about to receive a huge windfall of money?
- What should I be thinking about in order to financially navigate my divorce, the splitting of the household, and raising my kids alone?
- Should I save the money I got for my birthday or give it to a charity cause that I'm passionate about right now?
- Is this a lucky time to sell my house?
- Should I trust my friend with a loan?

Charts

The Buy-Sell Price Chart

This chart is designed to help you figure out what you need to know when offering a price for a purchase or when setting a price for a sale. It looks vaguely like a tree, so you can imagine it as a money tree. Runes should be cast up the tree to find out where they land. If you already have a specific price range in mind, you can limit the chart to the amounts you can manage. The point is not to have the runes tell you what to do but to allow some spiritual insight into a normally mundane and stressful process. Recall that runes have numerological meanings corresponding to their number in the alphabet, so these numbers can offer additional insights.

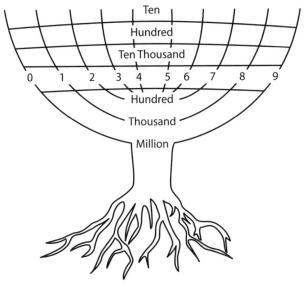

Buy-Sell Price Chart

Vision Board Chart

A vision board is a collection of images of what you want in life. The idea behind a vision board is that the more you think about and visualize the things you want happening, the more likely they are to manifest through a magical law called the law of attraction. The vision board chart pictured here is just an example of some material things people might want. Your own vision board will be highly individualized. If you want money to buy a professional makeup artist's kit and start your own salon, then you could draw the kit and your dream salon. If you want to buy a prize-winning racehorse, you could draw the horse being celebrated after a big win.

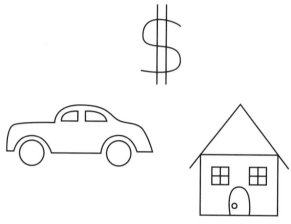

Vision Board Example

When casting the runes upon the chart, you'll be able to see advice that individual runes offer for how to achieve each goal. If runes that are unexpressed land on an image or if no runes land on an image, it means that you should focus on the other goals that do get a response from the runes. Note that there may be some negative runes that tell you where a problem lies and give you clues about how to fix such a problem.

Spreads
Save, Spend, Give Spread

1   2   3

I've used a simple three-rune spread for questions about balancing my budget. I've also used the three concepts as an image chart by drawing a red stop sign representing saving, a green arrow representing spending, and a smiling face representing giving to charity or to someone in need. It can help to cast the runes at random toward those images if I'm feeling lost about how to balance my financial activities. However, a spread is more useful advice for day to day, since I like to keep saving, spending, and giving to all in my life. Simply lay out a rune in a row for each of the options. Heed the advice the runes have to say about how you're balancing your budget.

For example, imagine drawing isa, algiz, and berkanan. If I drew these three, it would show me that my savings plan had essentially ground to a halt. Even if I am putting a certain amount every month into my savings account, it looks like my savings is not keeping up with the reality of the times and needs around me. I'd take the presence of isa to tell me that if I don't do anything, nothing will happen. This would encourage me to keep a stable savings plan and to not do anything wild with my savings for now. For my spending, algiz suggests a conservative approach, protecting my current investments without spending more except on things that directly serve my family and friends. For giving away, we see berkanan suggesting a nurturing means of giving. Perhaps this could mean donating to a food bank, or giving in a way that would see more growth, such as teaching elementary schoolers to knit hats for the homeless and buying yarn for the school. In general, this reading reflects careful saving and spending, as opposed to seeing a rune such as pertho that encourages more risk.

Problem-Solving Sword Spread

```
                6

    2     1       3       4

          5
```

When a specific financial problem comes up, the stress can be overwhelming. Perhaps you need to buy a car but can't see how to afford one. There are many options out there, and having too many options can be a pain to puzzle through. You might get a job with a better income and be able to afford a car, you might find a cheap car or even be given a fixer-upper by a friend, or you might find a better home location that eliminates your need for a car. There could be solutions out there that you haven't even thought about until the runes inspire your intuition.

The center rune at the hilt of the sword is read first as the situation. The rune to its left is read next as the past that led to this situation and potentially a mistake to be avoided in the future. The runes to the right represent the future if you continue on this present course and the likely outcome. The rune below this line represents some aid or hidden support. The rune above the line of runes represents a potential solution to the problem. You can lay out this spread multiple times to see multiple potential solutions if necessary. Normally, I don't recommend doing a rune reading on the same topic over and over again; that's just beating the dead horse, and I want you to actually use the advice you get from the runes the first time. A problem-solving spread such as this one is an exception to the rule of not doing repeated rune readings because the runes can help you gain perspective on multiple ways to solve the problem.

The positions on this sword teach you to think of how negative runes can be positive and positive runes can be negative. For example, if a "bad" rune such as hagalaz lands in the position of what will aid you or offer hidden support, it can mean that adversity helps change your perspective. You might be happier having enough money to survive, if not thrive, if you've managed to weather a major financial storm such as bankruptcy or a divorce. If a "good" rune such as wunjo is represented as the problem, it can help reveal something that you may have been willfully ignoring. For example, the presence of wunjo may mean that your Friday nights out with the girls are turning into an extra hundred dollars you can't afford to spend on your joy, so you should pick a more affordable hobby.

Rune Meanings in Context

Fehu: This is a very auspicious sign in a financial rune reading. There will be successful endeavors to work hard and earn sufficient money to thrive and share. Things will take time, however. Work on building a stable foundation, and you'll soon be able to afford bigger and better things.

Uruz: You're going to need to tough it out and power through a rough period financially. Though it may seem like unexpected car repair or medical bills keep coming out of nowhere, these obstacles can be overcome with your effort. Be assertive. If you're not getting the answers you need when playing phone tag with a question about a bill or a check, keep it up and be persistent.

Thurisaz: A lot of little money problems can add up to a big one. Perhaps your car gets a flat tire and forces you to take time off from paying work to fix it. Perhaps a simple habit like getting a specialty coffee every morning or smoking cigarettes is eating a hole in your pocketbook. The only way to strike down this giant is to keep your eye on your priorities and the long-term big picture.

Ansuz: You are about to receive good news financially, perhaps about an inheritance or loan coming through or about a debt being forgiven. Ansuz can also represent wise advice; maybe you should listen to what your parents have to say about buying a house, paying off your debt, avoiding credit cards, or starting a retirement plan.

Raido: Travel may lead to money. A more affordable cost of living may be found by moving to a new location. There may be a business trip in your future. Keep right on moving along. If a major setback happens, like being reported to a collection agency, don't get stuck wallowing in self-pity or fighting the powers that be. Keep your head high and keep working.

Ken: Your passions can lead to profit. Maybe you've always wanted to sell some handmade art online, to play music for money, or to go back to school to do what you really want to do in life. If you don't follow the call, your needs will lead to lackluster performance and earnings elsewhere in life. Even a small income from a hobby doesn't hurt.

Gebo: The generosity of others may lead to your financial benefit. A person-to-person loan may be forgiven, a large grant of money given, or there may be in-kind gifts of food and shelter when you are in need. This rune can also ask you to give until it hurts. A close friend or member of your community may be in need of your money or resources, or you may need to renew effort to collect donations for a favorite charity.

Wunjo: This rune is always good news, and it represents transcendent joy. A money problem will soon be solved, possibly by a windfall of money. It is also possible that you will merely release the stress of financial woes and find joy in the less tangible riches that you own. Either way, know that a sense of relief is in sight.

Hagalaz: Unexpected disaster may cause a huge problem with your household budget. Make sure that you have enough savings in the bank to carry you through a few months. Consider purchasing insurance to protect yourself against periods when you may be unable to work. Ensure that you're planning for your eventual retirement and potential living and health care needs after that.

Neid: Your basic needs must be met before anything else can be accomplished. Don't use avoidance to try to delay the inevitable duties that have to be done to provide for yourself. Wasting time hoping for a miracle instead of putting your nose to the grindstone may be an issue. Get your priorities straight and channel your funds toward your true needs.

Isa: Something has been blocked. If you're hoping for a check that is coming in the mail, it may have been lost. That loophole you've been trying to use to save you a lot of money is now closed. A vacation might need to be cancelled due to lack of funds. If you're working two jobs just to get by, the situation is rapidly becoming untenable.

Jera: This is a good sign for a gradual increase in income. A new job opportunity or money-saving, shared-living situation with friends or family may open up some distance from you, but the move or commute is worth it. Now is a good time for investing in an education. Learning more about things like stocks, bonds, and mutual funds may allow you to navigate them successfully for profit.

Eihwaz: Your money situation as it exists now may continue in this manner for quite some time, so I hope you're sitting pretty. If you're going through tough times, don't ease up yet. If you're doing pretty well for yourself, you can rest assured that you're unlikely to get suddenly fired or have something horribly expensive happen soon, so it's a good time to put extra money in savings for a rainy day.

Pertho: A risk needs to be taken, but it is a necessary risk. Investments that are potentially risky will pay off. If you have the entertainment budget, the purchase of a lottery ticket may even be in order. Trust that if you invest the time in a new money-making endeavor, it has a high potential to pay off. Creative use of finances may lead to contentment.

Algiz: This is a saving rune, and it asks you to invest in things that protect you. Doublecheck to make sure that your home, vehicles, and business have the right insurance. Your loyalty will pay off. Now is not the time to switch jobs or banks. Look into businesses that reward you for your loyalty, and you can find a lot of unexpected savings.

Sowilo: Success can be had with your financial endeavor. This is a good sign if you're asking whether to start a business or new job or buy a house or car. Even if times are troubled, this is a reassuring sign that all of your stress now will pay off. Eventual success can be had. Make sure that you're balancing your investments or your budget, as this rune can sometimes lend hyperfocused energy.

Tiwaz: If you've been tempted to obtain money in ways that are less than ethical or legal, think again. It is time to go the traditional route whenever possible. If you're hoping to start a zany side business, now is not the right time. Later in life may be the time to pursue eccentric possibilities, but for now keep your eyes straight ahead.

Berkanan: A new project may lead to abundant riches. If you want to have success, you'll need to carefully nurture your savings. Choose safe and stable investments at this time, and instead think of slow growth of your assets. Notice if anything in your life has been stifled or cut off by lack of funds and then budget for the important things in life.

Ehwaz: You can't do this alone. You have to be resourceful and to reach out to those who can help you. Taking help as it is offered is not the same as being a freeloader, so get rid of your guilt. You're part of a community, and that means sharing needs to happen. Consider taking on a roommate or accepting the offer of a family member to give you a loan or a job.

Mannaz: Your financial woes are all in your head. Look at your financial situation from the perspective of an outside observer to reduce anxiety. Smart investments are needed, so try talking with a financial planner or taking a class on managing money. You'll need to strategize and make a plan in order to achieve your goals because force of will alone won't do it this time.

Laguz: Money is an emotional issue for you right now, so be careful that you don't start having arguments with a significant other or family member about financial stability and smart purchases. It could be that your emotions are getting the better of you. Put away that credit card and delay any major purchases for a while until you can assess your true reasons for buying.

Ingwaz: Now is a good time to sign any financial agreement. Sign that lease or talk to that lawyer about protecting your finances from any impending battles. You'll soon find some relative stability in your finances. There may be a very good partnership forming. This is a good sign for couples who are just getting started sharing accounts, rent payments, or other assets and obligations.

Othila: Real estate is a key resource for you right now. If you haven't yet owned your first home, now is the time to look into buying a place or look into any inheritable property you might one day own. If you do own a home, focus your efforts on investing in your home. Fix anything that hasn't been fixed for a while. Make any major replacements or repairs at home.

Dagaz: You need to cut off something or someone that is draining your bank account. Perhaps you have a subscription to service that you no longer need. Maybe that class or hobby really isn't serving you anymore, and it's time to sell all equipment and be done with it. If you have a family member who is old enough and able enough to work for himself or herself, it is time for some tough love.

The Blank Rune: Money is running out for a project in your life. Cut your losses and move on, because you can't know enough about the situation to take a calculated risk. Stop trying to see the future of your money for now. It's time to either outsource your money management to a professional or more knowledgeable person.

Career and School

Just last month I performed a career rune reading for a client who had previously had a love rune reading from me and was particularly happy with the results. She was more than willing to try the runes again and ready to trust the answers they gave about her career path. I hadn't seen this client in quite a while, and the last time she had been in college for a business degree. I expressed congratulations when she told me that she had graduated, but she confessed that she decided a business career wasn't for her.

Over the past year and a half she had tried working for several major corporations and got a bad taste in her mouth for business in general. The subject she found so interesting in school now seemed boring and superficial. She quit her business jobs and took up a part-time job at a gym, teaching yoga to seniors to make ends meet. She said that teaching yoga was okay, but she wasn't really passionate about it or making nearly enough money.

She had several ideas for what to do with her career going forward. The first option she thought about was starting her own yoga business, buying a studio, and training employees. The second option she thought about was going back to school to become a physical therapist, since she had heard conversations at the gym that led her to believe physical therapists make lots of money, and she really did enjoy working with people.

I decided to do three separate three-rune readings for her. One to explore the potential of the yoga business idea, one to show what her life would look like if she chose to get a physical therapy degree instead, and one to see anything else the runes had to reveal, like perhaps a third option of a totally different career. As I explained the meanings of each rune to her, we both noticed how much more positive the runes were about the potential of going back to school than the yoga business idea. The extra rune reading added some insight that made me modify the recommendation to go back to school. The runes pointed out that her ability to counsel people and offer encouragement were outstanding and suggested that she build knowledge upon her business degree rather than casting it aside. I asked if she had ever considered getting a degree in psychology or marriage and family therapy instead. She was excited about that idea and enthusiastic about how her business skills could help her found her own private practice as a therapist.

I've seen runes encourage teachers to get started working with children, and I've seen runes confirm when it's time to retire and work out of desire instead of out of necessity. There's something that speaks viscerally to one who puts faith in a spiritual tool for mapping out a major life path such as career. Many of my clients are university students because college is an anxious time in which so many resources are being spent on what for some people could turn out to be essentially an exploratory guess about one's destiny. When choosing your own destiny, use the runes to paint a picture of what you see. The meanings of the runes have been generalized, in some cases since ancient times when the economy looked much different. There are some personality traits, such as work ethic, that remain true of some people throughout history. Gather your runes and start to think intelligently about the career path you've mapped out for your life.

Expectations

Remember that you are in charge of your own destiny, and the runes aren't meant to be random lots cast to saddle you with a specific career label. I remember that when I was first starting college, I figured one major would lead to a very specific career. As I grew older, I learned that even very disparate skills can mesh together to form a firm foundation for a flexible career path. In a workplace, many people will have different backgrounds. Instead of thinking of your school or career path as having one final destination, imagine that you're busy building the best foundation you can for a jumping-off point to the rest of your life. Here are some questions you can ask to gain the guidance you need:

- Which of these two jobs will ultimately be best for myself and my family?
- What should I be thinking about when choosing a college that is right for me?
- What sort of work will help me survive and thrive?
- Which of these two majors would be a smart choice for gaining the most marketable skills?
- Should I pursue my passion or should I do what is expected of me?

- Is now the right time to retire?
- Is my business idea financially viable?
- Can I trust my new boss?

Charts

"Am I on the Right Track?" Chart

Essentially, what most people want to know when they reach for the runes with a career or school question is whether it's best to stay the course or to change directions and try a new approach. This chart is simply a depiction of a bridge that shows whether this path you are choosing is a permanent one or one on which you will need to retrace your steps. The bridge is a powerful symbol that represents transition. You've heard of the cliché of "burning bridges," in which you cross a bridge and cannot cross back. The imagery of the bridge helps tell you how much you've invested in your current career or school track and whether you should continue on this path.

The trick to this casting is to divide all the runes into two equal handfuls without looking at them and then to cast them on either side of the bridge at once. The runes that you selected for the left-hand side of the bridge will likely fall around the left side and those you selected for the right bank of the bridge will likely fall to the right, but it's okay and expected that there be some crossover. The left-hand side of the bridge represents what supports you, where you're coming from, and your current situation. The runes on the right side of the bridge represent the future of this particular path. Runes that fall below the bridge represent underlying emotions, since water is symbolic of feelings. Runes that fall above the bridge represent communications and thoughts about the path. Runes that fall on the bridge itself represent physical manifestations of actual events that can come about from this career or school path.

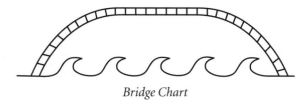

Bridge Chart

For example, ehwaz in the past may represent loyalty to an old job and staying the course in your career. However, if it falls in the water instead, it might mean that you have to seek the source of that feeling not in your literal past but in your roots. Perhaps the rune speaks to a childhood career dream of becoming a firefighter or doctor. Perhaps the rune is connected to a parent's career and represents taking over your father's insurance agency once he retires. Keep in mind that all of the runes could potentially be displayed in this chart casting method. In practice, of course, many of the runes land facedown and remain unexpressed.

Elemental Career or College Major Match Chart

Figuring out your ideal college major or career role can and should be like administering a personality test to yourself. Some careers have aspects to them that fit your style, while other aspects of the job are deal-breakers. For example, I would love to be a midwife because I'm not squeamish, I'd love taking more schooling to be medically trained, and it sounds fascinating to help mothers bring babies into the world. But I need my sleep, and babies don't always come at convenient times. Being a midwife is definitely not the right career for me. I landed on the role of being a fortune-teller, and it's the perfect job for me. When I performed a rune reading many years ago, before I went to college, and checked my career path, the runes suggested that I would be drawn to teaching. While it's true that I did get my masters in teaching and taught children for a while, I now realize that my role as a teacher extends into my work as an author and my work with fortune-telling apprentices. Even my vocation as the mother of my children leads me back to teaching.

Elemental Chart

The elemental chart helps you understand your personality characteristics by dividing them into the four classical elements. Cast the runes onto the chart. If most runes fall in the air category, it suggests you might be working with technology or communications. Lawyers and other people who work with ideas are people with careers associated with the air element. Look at the runes that are there for further detail. For example, if neid shows up, you know that you might be involved with emergency communications or crisis counseling. If raido makes an appearance, your communications job will involve long-distance communications, perhaps as a translator, for example.

If most runes fall into the fire category, they indicate a creative passion or art. The runes that fall in this section can also be interpreted as your passions if you have trouble figuring out what your passions are yourself. It's perfectly understandable to try to use the runes to get in touch with your passions on an intellectual level. Here are some examples of rune interpretations as they fall in the fire category: If hagalaz appears, you know that the creative passion will also have an element of pain or destruction, such as a career as a plastic surgeon. If you see fehu, you may be one of the lucky few to actually make money creating art such as pottery.

Runes that fall in the water category show what brings you emotional fulfillment. Counselors and doctors are often associated with the water element. Don't underestimate how important it is to feel emotionally complete from your work here on earth. It's not enough to merely love your job. If you work as a professional kitten wrangler and have fun all day at your job but find yourself feeling unhappy with the lack of significance of your work, you might be emotionally unfulfilled and thus sabotage your work to get out of your job.

Finally, the earth category of runes holds the most interesting information because it shows how your job will manifest in the physical world. Jobs for people with most runes in the earth category include those that involve working with your hands or body, such as a fitness instructor or a craftsperson. However, it is fun to use your intuition to try to puzzle out what sort of job you will have from what runes do land in this area of the chart, even if there are just a few. Ask yourself what sorts of roles in the real world around you fit the characteristics of the runes you see in the earth quadrant of this chart. Think literally when interpreting runes in this section. For example, sowilo might mean work as a lighting technician for a theater or movie set, while uruz may mean using your brute strength as a laborer or bodyguard.

Spreads

The Job Hunt Spread

5	6	7	8	9	10	11
		2	3	4		
			1			

Many of the clients who come to me for a reading are anxiously navigating a job hunt. They want to know about what sort of job will be landed and when, and what can be done to hasten the successfulness of the job hunt. This spread looks like an inverted triangle. The bottom rune is laid out first and represents the physical manifestation of the job. If you need a better analysis of what your career will be like, use the Elemental Career or College Major Match Chart.

The next row of three runes in the triangle spread tells you the past, present, and future of this particular job hunt. The row that shows your progress can be especially helpful if you're looking at one particular job application and tracking its progress. The final row has seven runes and is all about timing. The seven runes represent the seven days of the week, starting with the day it is today and ending with the seventh day in the future from today. In addition, this row should be carefully interpreted numerologically to investigate the potential of years, months, or days of the month in the future. For example, if for Monday you see fehu, it could mean that you find success with a job on Monday. Since fehu is also the number one, if you rule out Monday as a possibility, you can still welcome the first of the month and January, the first month of the year, as auspicious times for finding a job.

Interpersonal Work Issues Spread

2

1

3   4

The example spread above involves you and three coworkers. This spread is made like a wheel, and the number of spokes of the wheel depends on the number of people in your workplace that you'd like to investigate. The axle of the wheel represents yourself as all the people in your work perceive you to be. Each of the spokes of the wheel are people at your work. Choose the people associated with each spoke as you draw and place the runes. The position of each person around the wheel is arbitrary, and you can decrease or increase the number of spokes as needed. The runes as you lay them down represent that person's feelings and intentions toward you. So far, we've just been placing spokes on the wheel, but you can expand your readings as you become more experienced. A ring around the wheel, outside the spokes, represents how the different people that you're investigating interact with each other in a way that pertains to you. The wheel formation of this spread is especially helpful if you're looking at whether people in your workplace are conspiring behind the scenes to fire or promote you.

Let's take a look at a practical example of this spread. James is a client who has been experiencing frustrations with too many changes at work. We'll draw a rune for James and place it in the middle of everything. We draw uruz, which is a positive rune showing that he has a good work ethic. However, James complains that his boss, Susan, doesn't appreciate his work as a retail store manager. Susan has brought in David to rearrange the store's displays to make it look cuter and more like a boutique. This meddling irritates James and his assistant manager Lisa. We draw ehwaz for Lisa, hagalaz for David, and pertho for Susan. Lisa is clearly a loyal friend; however, her loyalty might not be enough in this case. Susan is taking risks with her business and is using David to shake things up. The whole situation looks very unstable, so James would be foolish to make a stand in this case. I would advise James to either allow himself to be transformed, or to take the reins in his own hands and resign before things change so much that they become unbearable.

Rune Meanings in Context

Fehu: Your work is viewed favorably by others. In fact, there may be some people at your workplace or past workplace who are fighting hard in your favor to allow you to be rewarded with the compensation that you deserve. You have skills that are of value to a company. Allow yourself to be viewed as an asset and ask potential employers why you should choose them over others.

Uruz: Be forceful with your needs. If you are applying for a job, don't be afraid to call and follow up, asking, "Have you had a chance to look over my résumé today?" Your persistence and assertiveness will be viewed positively instead of as a nuisance. If you already have a job, there may be some unexpected misfortune due to the economy or other forces at large, but you can power through it and remain on top.

Thurisaz: Someone or some situation at work is out to get you. There might be a coworker who is a thorn in your side, a boss with a personality conflict, or a storm brewing in your workplace that will lead to layoffs in the future. Don't ignore the nagging annoyances, as they are signs that you must change your entire work environment.

Ansuz: You're hearing a divine calling to a vocation. Do not ignore your dreams, as you will only be drawn back to them over and over again no matter what you do. Seek wise advice and give your dreams your best shot, even if they seem wild or unprofitable. You may find that this path is a stepping-stone to something greater.

Raido: Just keep moving through the problems you face. If you're a student dreading finals week, whatever the outcome, know that it will all be over soon. If you are applying for jobs and getting nothing in reply, keep up the good work of applying but expand your reach to greater distances away from the locations you've been scouting so far.

Ken: This is a very auspicious rune for those who are students, because it represents the fire of passion for knowledge. Find what lights a fire in you to know more and pursue that education relentlessly. In the workplace, this rune shows that your voice needs to be heard in order to solve a major problem. If you are ignored, there may be some serious internal upset, interpersonally within the workplace or within yourself personally.

Gebo: Expect a generous wage increase. Now is an auspicious time to ask for a raise or to seek out a job that rewards you more appropriately for the work you do. For students, this rune represents an opportunity falling in your lap to volunteer or take on an internship that can change your life and your career path.

Wunjo: This rune is a promotion rune and represents cause for celebration. You will pass a test, achieve a new job position, or celebrate new opportunities and responsibilities. Make sure to thank all the people who got you to where you are. Set new and even more ambitious goals.

Hagalaz: Destruction is coming. Your workplace may be reorganizing and laying off people, including yourself. Interpersonal conflict may find you losing your job. If you're a student, an unexpected health, financial, or personal issue may cause you to have to drop out of a lot of classes at once or take a hit on your grade.

Neid: You are not having your needs fulfilled at your current place of work. If you're a student, you are lacking some key background knowledge and your current school program may not be the one to fulfill your requirements. If you are working, your job or business idea is not giving you enough to pay the bills. Fall back on another job or helpful people in order to stay afloat.

Isa: You're stuck in a dead-end job. There is nothing that you can do to cajole your boss into promoting you or allowing your situation to change for the better. Backtracking may be the only key tactic here. If you're a student, you may be in the wrong major. It can be frustrating to start all over again, but it is better to double back now than years down the road.

Jera: Success can be had on this career path, but it is a long road. You'll need to invest some time, effort, and even travel into your career path. A serious course of study may need to be undertaken to improve your career. The good news is that you'll be studying something you already know and improving upon skills you already have.

Eihwaz: You're about to come to a breakthrough point in your career, but the change will come from a philosophical place from within you rather than from external circumstances and simply being given a good job. You may come to find that a service-oriented volunteer opportunity, internship, or mindset in your job right now will help change attitudes of those around you.

Pertho: The job hunt may be a numbers game for you right now. Apply for as many jobs as possible, so that you have several offers to sift through. For students, this rune asks you to explore all the passions you can in your schooling. If you have an opportunity to minor in another specialty or to take classes that are outside of your normal focus, it is okay to take the risk.

Algiz: Your network of friends will be vital to your career success. Ask for favors or for introductions to influential people. Someone in your workplace may be looking out for you and protecting you. Now is the time to forge strong and long-lasting alliances that can aid you in your career. If you're dealing with a rival in your career or education, be firm and unyielding. Follow procedures to the letter in order to catch cheaters in the act.

Sowilo: This rune is a sure sign of success. You will have an opportunity to let yourself shine. If you are a student, this may be an opportunity to help write a published paper or give an important talk. If you are in your career, you have the chance to represent your organization or to show off a project that has been your baby. Use this moment to slingshot your career higher, because your work is being viewed in a very favorable light.

Tiwaz: Be careful to follow the rules if you are starting a business, and don't deviate too far from the beaten path. If you're a student, stay on your current choice of study, and know that your work will be challenging but possible. There may be some conflicts in the workplace, but you can steadfastly prove that you are the one in the right with logic, facts, and proof.

Berkanan: A major work project has the potential to pay off with abundant wealth. This rune is a very good sign for those who are running their own businesses, because it shows how the project they've nurtured is growing. For students, this rune also encourages a project-based approach, implying it may be time to choose a capstone project, thesis, or dissertation.

Ehwaz: This rune is an excellent sign for a business partnership, showing an alliance that can be trusted to bring profit. If you're wondering whether to choose a specific job offer or school that has offered enrollment to you, this rune tells you to go for it. Seek out those partners who have helped you along the way, whether they be recruiters, academic advisors, or supervisors, and solidify those networking bonds. Someone with whom you work may invite you in on a side project, different job, or business opportunity.

Mannaz: Look at the bigger picture of your work situation to see why your organization is handling things the way that it is. A simple shift of the frame of mind may be what is needed. This rune usually means that you should stay the course and not make major changes. Look at how an outsider would view your work and allow your attitude to adjust.

Laguz: This is a very positive rune to find in a career reading because it indicates that your job position is protected from harm. This rune also encourages you to do the work that you truly love. Strive to allow yourself more creativity in your school or work. You need an appropriate emotional outlet in your daily duties. Talk to the people in power to find out whether flexibility, creativity, or delegating work to others will allow you some emotional relief.

Ingwaz: This rune indicates a harmonious business merger. If you own your own business, this rune is an auspicious sign and encourages you to trust a potential partnership. If you work for an organization, this rune can cause a little anxiety because changes will happen during the process of forming new alliances, but all should work out for the best. If you are a student, this rune indicates that you must reach out to another organization, perhaps for school credit or padding on your résumé as well as for making connections useful for your future.

Othila: This rune asks for you to focus on the physical assets associated with your work. If you own a business or work for a company, this rune draws your focus to the property, inventory, and fixed assets. If you are a student, this rune asks you to make connections and apply for jobs right where you are or where your roots are based. Look for runes near this one to see whether there are problems with the present organization or if the rune is simply asking you to add to what is already there.

Dagaz: You are coming to a stage of completion of your degree, certification, or job role. You must think about the next steps in your career. Let go of anything that is finished, even if you have an emotional attachment to a defunct project, a school campus, or even a colleague who is simply no longer doing his or her job competently. You can move on to something bigger and better once you allow the sun to set on this stage of your career.

The Blank Rune: There's not enough information available for you to proceed in this situation. If you're thinking of starting a business, I'm afraid it's simply not going to get off the ground. Be careful about a career or school opportunity that may turn out to be a scam. If somebody is asking you to invest time or money in something that will pay off, it may be that the necessary collateral is not there. Be very conservative.

four

Tapping into the Power of Runes

It was the week of my dad's surgery. I'd never really known anyone so close to me who had cancer before. As I struggled to sleep with all of these thoughts swirling around in my brain, my gods sent me a wonderful dream in which I drew an empowering runic talisman to protect my father from all of the fears of the unknown associated with his surgery. When I awoke, I felt like I'd had an epiphany. I knew my father was not a religious man, so he would never appreciate an organized prayer circle the same way such a gesture would comfort me. But, as it happens, my dad was a big believer in good luck charms. Whenever he would go gambling in a casino, he would be extremely wary of any jinx that might cause a streak of bad luck and would gravitate toward things he deemed lucky. So I asked whether he would like to have a good luck charm for surgery. He agreed, so I set about making him a runic good luck charm. The process of creating the charm helped me feel less helpless against my imagination-fuelled fears and gave my dad a tool to allay his own valid worries surrounding his cancer treatment.

Here are some more examples of how runes can provide spiritual support using some of my favorite runes. As I was in the course of writing this book, there was a terrible terrorist event that drew the world's eye to several countries in peril. A friend of mine asked me if there was some kind of peace meditation that she could use with the runes. I drew a wheel of runes that looked like a mandala for her to meditate on for peace. In the center, I featured laguz, representing love flowing from within the individual meditating. In the second ring of the wheel, I repeated the rune ansuz, representing this love communicated out into the world and arising spontaneously from that divine place within others. On the external part of the wheel I wrote the rune othila representing the love and peace radiating outward and then returning inward to alleviate the suffering in my friend's heart. I instructed her to meditate upon the wheel daily after lighting a white candle for peace at 7 p.m. so that we could do the meditation together even when apart. Making the rune wheel also helped me process my own feelings about what was happening in the news. After all, making a runic wheel has a great element of artistry to it. There are so many different ways to arrange the runes to create an effect, and you'll have to use some trial and error to sense whether the resulting design feels right to you. In the process of making my art, I was able to express my own feelings as well as to do something creative and positive with those sad feelings instead of just moping around.

Another friend of mine wrote to me this week asking for prayer and guidance. She has been embroiled in a custody battle over her daughter for some time after a heartbreaking divorce from her high school sweetheart. Unfortunately, she made the situation worse when she got snippy as her ex-husband's new wife was dropping off my friend's daughter. In the rage of the moment, my friend called the woman a nasty name in front of her young daughter and immediately regretted it. She e-mailed me asking for prayer to stop any repercussions from affecting her daughter negatively. She feared that her daughter would learn bad habits and also that the custody battle would become more mean-spirited. I suggested that my friend send the woman she wronged a gift card or some flowers with an apology to try to smooth things over. Meanwhile, she and her daughter could make a charm for her daughter's backpack that carried algiz. My friend could explain to her daughter that the rune represents protection and her parents' love for her, which she carries with her wherever she goes, even when parents make mistakes. Meanwhile, my friend could sing ansuz in prayer to ask the divine for guidance helping her communicate with her daughter's other family in a way that comes from a place of love instead of fear and anger.

When I was a teenager, I used runes to perform a special ritual that I used to attune myself to the divine. I wanted to dedicate myself to my spiritual path, but I was at a loss as to how to do so. I was too young to seek formal training as any sort of clergy, but I felt like I was coming home into my religion of choice and I wanted to mark the transition point with a dedication ceremony. I drew a rune to see whether it was time to perform the ritual for myself and I ended up with othila, which cemented for me the idea that I was finding names for the gods and religion to which I had felt called for my entire life. I chose a special spiritual name for myself and wrote it out in runes in my new spiritual journal. Then, under the light of the moon and stars, I introduced myself to the four directions using my new spiritual name. I knelt down and curved my body around so that I took roughly the shape of othila. Placing one hand on my head and the other on the bottom of my foot, I told the world that everything between my two hands now belonged to my gods. It was a simple ritual, and I'm sure that I only looked crudely like a rune, but the feeling that I evoked at that time will stay with me for a lifetime.

Runes are one of the most fulfilling of divinatory tools because they are satisfying and easy to handle. Connecting runes with deeper spiritual practices in your life will make you a better fortune-teller for several reasons. First, you'll be adding deeper meaning to your inner rune lexicon. If all you've ever known about runes comes from a book, you can certainly begin a competent rune-reading practice. However, if you've had a life-changing spiritual experience during a meditation, dream, or prayer in which the rune appeared to you in a dazzling vision, you'll have a more significant personal attachment to that rune. You'll never forget a rune's meaning if it is solidified by a powerful spiritual experience. This chapter is all about diving deep into the power of the runes.

Ancient peoples used runes not only for divination and as a written script but in daily spiritual life as well. In modern times it can be difficult to wrap one's head around the subtly spiritual meanings of each rune since not many of us are trained in spiritual vocations. Each of the runes can be used to describe spiritual experiences and theological concepts that the English language doesn't always have a single word equivalent to describe. The world of the ancient people was full of spiritual mysteries, entities, and specters, each of which had finely nuanced mythologies reflected in the runes. While many of the original meanings may be lost forever to time, a modern spiritual person can make personal discoveries with runes that enrich and develop his or her world.

In this chapter, I'd like to show you some ancient tips and techniques that have worked for me. I like to call these "rules" simply because they have been observed over time to work for myself and many others in general. However, the ancient gods are not leaning over you and enforcing these rules of the runes, so if some of them don't work for you, you're welcome to make up rules of your own as you go along. Not all the following techniques are possible to employ with every rune application, so just aim for as many as practical, or for just the ones that make sense to you. For the beginner, it can be helpful to follow established modes of practice, but we're all making new discoveries as we go along. Let's start out with some basic concepts that have come down to us through the ages and still have great applications today.

Knowings

A knowing is an important tool when using runes to conceptualize a spiritual desire, person, or object. The word "knowing," as used in the context of modern rune practices, derives from the Norse *kenning*. Essentially, a kenning is a poetic name for something. For use with runes, a knowing is a true name given to a magical tool or object or a way to describe an intent or desire. Typically, knowings are written on a sacred object, but they can also be sung, prayed, or used as a spiritual nickname. Modern magical practitioners believe that if you know the true name of something, you have power over it. So when creating a sacred object, naming a place of spiritual significance, choosing a spiritual name for yourself, or even wording a prayer, you should be careful about naming your desire. The ideal name should be beautiful, awe inspiring, and rich with imagery and should roll off the tongue.

In ancient times, instead of simply calling a sword "my sword," a warrior would give that sword a poetic name like "He strikes fear in enemies," "Blood paints him and protects my family," or "Dances in light so quickly my opponent can't see." Each name could be the line in a poem, evoking visual imagery that makes the weapon more than just a tool. Likewise, a runemaster might choose a poetic name like "She who serves Freya through song" or "He who heals with staves." Feel free to get as poetic and abstract as you like when crafting your own knowings, and experiment with giving magical objects a true name the way the ancients did.

A knowing is the first step when you have a spiritual need that you want to address through runes. When you have a problem that you want to solve through meditation, prayer, or magic, think carefully about the result that you want to achieve. Come up with a knowing that describes the ultimate achievement of that spiritual goal. Use your creativity and imagination to express your spiritual goal in a poetic way. For example, if you want your knees to heal after surgery, your knowing might be phrased "I bow gracefully and joyfully before the gods." If you need to discover a new and peaceful place to live, your knowing for that need might be "I am a boat guided gently through the storm to my home." If you need to work more efficiently at your job, your knowing might sound like "My hands work quickly, like spiders weaving webs, to bring wealth to my family."

The next step is to turn your knowing into a line of runes. Since rune staves have traditionally been written on things when using them spiritually, the following steps will assume that's what you're doing. When writing runes for spiritual purposes, the ancient peoples who wrote them may have preferred to use as few runes as possible and use abbreviations whenever possible. In fact, when ancient peoples wrote out their knowings, they did not use any spaces or punctuation, which makes older runic inscriptions sort of hard to read. They also spelled words phonetically, so you'll want to take care to spell out English words phonetically using the sounds of the runes rather than finding equivalents to every letter. For example, the key sounds in "I love you" would be rendered "I luv yu" in runes.

They also used the runes as pictograms whenever possible to compress the meanings further. So instead of writing "man rides horse," ancient peoples might use the runes mannaz, raido, and ehwaz written all together without spaces between them, each one acting as a pictogram for a word in the knowing. Ancient peoples believed that condensing the rune meanings to pictograms was the most powerful way to use them. It's important to write out your runes carefully so that there is a beginning, a middle, and an end to every rune "sentence" even if your runes are used only as pictograms. Think to yourself whether the first rune is how you want the situation to start and whether the last rune you write is how you want the outcome to appear. If you find your beginning and ending runes lacking, reorganize your knowing.

When making the final draft of your knowing for your journal, as a meditative focus, or on a talisman, carve each rune individually, even if some of the staves overlap visually. If you are carving in wood, for example, run your blade again over areas that have been previously carved if they are part of a stave that you are adding to a bindrune.

Bindrunes

One way to combine and condense runes even further is to essentially write the runes on top of one another to create a "bindrune" so that they have a new, compound meaning. Bindrunes can be elegant and beautiful in appearance. Since ancient peoples didn't really pay attention to which way the staves were facing when they carved them, you can take similar liberties and flip runes around until they look beautiful when melded together. You can write out an entire knowing as a bindrune, or you can use bindrunes sparingly when writing out a line of runes in order to combine certain concepts so that they are more powerful and make more sense to you. For example, if you were making a bindrune to help a soldier come home from a war, you might choose to combine tiwaz with mannaz to represent the soldier and then othila to represent the soldier's homecoming. Depending on how the bindrune looks and feels to you, you can optionally put all three staves together or simply combine the first two and add more onto the sentence to clarify your wishes for the solider if your knowing has more complex and poetic meanings to express.

A useful example of a bindrune that you can adapt to your own needs is to make a bindrune that means "protection (against something)" by beginning with algiz and then adding a rune to represent your specific protection needs. For example, anyone could use protection against disrupting circumstances, represented by hagalaz. But when traveling through the desert, one might want protection against the hot sun, represented by sowilo. A person struggling with a gambling addiction might want protection against pertho. As you construct a simple knowing for protection, get as specific as you want with your protection needs and then choose the rune that represents the greater category that encompasses that need.

Once you've settled on a rune combination, get out some scratch paper and try combining the runes in different ways that look pretty. As you do so, you may notice that new runes seem to appear as you connect the stave lines. Look for hidden runes that may compromise or enhance your meaning. For example, if you accidentally find that two runes lean together to form uruz, that's actually a good thing. Uruz can add power to any bindrune. However, other runes might confuse your meaning, so take care to select a different orientation of your runes or even separate them out if necessary. A clearer meaning of your runes is more important than a condensed one, especially for a beginner. If you find yourself thinking about an alternate meaning of your rune combination every time you look at them, your intention will be misdirected, and as a result you might cause unintended changes in your world.

Carving Runes

Traditionally, the first step to bringing spiritual life to the runes is to carve them. Indeed, the evidence we have of the spiritual use of runes comes from magical objects onto which the runes were carved. Rune staves can be carved into traditional metal tools, wooden or stone plaques, or jewelry. You can carve runes into anything, however, and our modern lives provide opportunities for carving runes everywhere and anywhere. You can scratch rune staves on your cell phone if you want to receive good news.

My favorite simple application is to carve runes that I want to embody onto the peel of a banana. My husband always wonders how I eat so many bananas, but I'm pretty addicted to them as a healthy breakfast food and snack. I carve staves directly onto the banana, still in the peel, with a toothpick or a paperclip bent straight, so the carving is just a scratch and doesn't go all the way through to the fruit. Overnight, the carving turns black and contrasts impressively against the yellow peel, which makes it appear as though the runes have been empowered. I then eat the fruit mindfully during the day when I have need of the runes' influence, or add it to my breakfast smoothie to power me throughout my day.

It's not always practical to carve runes. You might not want to mar the surface of a car you want to empower with runes. However, whenever it is possible and practical to carve or scratch runes into a surface, it is advisable to do so. The act of carving, if even in token, is a symbolic way to alter the universe around you. As you create the runes, you destroy, and this duality reflects the mysteries of manifestation.

Reading Runes as Script

Reading the runes that you write is vital to acknowledging their power. As anyone who has seen a bad tattoo will tell you, proofreading your runes is crucial. A bad tattoo is forever, but so is a misspelled rune if you go through the process of spiritually giving it your intention and manifesting change in your universe. For this reason, it's worth your time as a beginner to work on learning to read rune letter rows as a script in addition to learning their divinatory meanings. Luckily, several of the runes look quite a bit like the English letters for the sounds they represent. You can practice using runes as a script in your everyday life if you'd like to become more familiar with reading them.

As you view your runes at this stage, you don't need to read them aloud. That part comes later. This moment is all about visualization and committing your thoughts to memory. To read your runes, merely gaze upon the staves and read them carefully and with intention. If you've written a bindrune, allow your mind to process each rune in order, forcing them to pop out one at a time in your mind's eye as you look upon the bindrune. Try to mentally read the runes in this way each time you look at the bindrune from now on, rather than seeing them as the design you arranged as a whole. Though the design of the bindrune is important for catching your eye and allowing it to wander as if it is in a labyrinth, the bindrune should always hold meaning in your mind and not recede into your memory as an abstract work of art.

I love to write using runes as a spiritual practice. At first it can be a challenge, but soon it can become a meditative trance exercise. Learning to use a new script to write is very difficult, so don't get frustrated with yourself if you can't scribble out a page of rune notes in as much time as you can write in cursive. At first, writing a script can feel like solving a puzzle as you work to encrypt your writing. Choose a favorite poem or prayer and sink into the process. Sound out each word and search for the best runes to fit. As you write, let the ideas associated with each runic pictogram flash through your mind and have fun trying to make connections with the word you're writing. Before long, you'll find the process of writing with runes gets faster and faster, as you start to memorize the most common runes. You'll become comfortable with them and able now to take this internalized knowledge of the runes back to your readings with runes.

Writing with runes in a script can safeguard private, sacred text from the casual observer's prying eyes. When I moved out of my childhood home and went off to college, I suddenly found myself living in a group dorm room cluster where privacy was nonexistent. I began writing private spiritual things using the script Runes of Honorius, also known as Theban. Important dates for full moon meditations or for meeting up with like-minded folks were written in this script so that my roommates didn't ask personal questions and didn't get spooked by a roommate engaged in witchcraft. I assume they simply thought I was writing in another language, and my plan worked perfectly to keep my sacred things to myself.

Painting or Staining Runes

Even if your runic spiritual exercise creates only temporary writing, such as writing runes on a piece of paper that is to be burned in a fire, the act of adding color and filling in grooves made by carving is a symbolic one. Painting can add additional meaning through associations you make with the color. So for runes painted for love, passion, or war, you can use the color red. Refer to "How to Make Runes" in chapter 6 for a list of some of my color associations as examples.

After the act of destruction by carving the runes, painting or staining them is creativity at work. When I paint runes that have been cut into wood, it often feels as if I'm applying a healing salve to the wounds in the tree branch. Painting the staves builds upon what you have destroyed but makes your marks more vibrant instead of covering them up. So too are your wishes imprinted more firmly in the universe by painting or staining runes after cutting them, whenever possible and practical.

Charging Your Runes

To "charge" an object means to imbue it with spiritual energy. Of course, spiritual energy is not the same as electrical energy, so you won't be charging your runes like you charge your electronic devices. Spiritual energy is more about making a connection with the ritual object and initiating the movement of your emotions, desires, and that spiritual energy toward manifestation out in the universe.

Before you charge your runes, first think about how you sense spiritual energy. When you purchased your runes, did you run your hands over several sets of runes? What did you feel? If you haven't felt energy before, keep in mind that it can feel different to different people. Some people visualize energy in the mind's eye as a light or flowing colors surrounding the object. Some people have a tactile sense of energy as a sensation of warmth, coolness, pressure, tingling, or fuzziness. One or more of these ways to detect energy might come into play when you are charging your runes and deciding when you are finished charging them.

Step 1: Hold the intention that you have for your runes clearly in your mind. Allow yourself to evoke emotions associated with your goal as if the goal had already been achieved. Some people find that visualization helps to raise the appropriate energy. So if you were charging runes to heal a broken leg, visualize the person joyfully moving about after being completely healed, and try to experience the happiness you would feel by seeing that person feeling all right again. If you are charging an object to protect your home, imagine a scenario in which you have successfully warded off potential danger from your home and allow yourself to feel the protective mama bear emotions you might feel, perhaps as you righteously watch would-be robbers hauled away by police.

Step 2: Pick up the object upon which you've placed your runes and will your visualizations and emotions into the object. You can visualize your spiritual energy as a light imbuing the object with power, or simply squeeze the object tightly and hope with all your heart. As you do so, intone the sound that the rune letter makes, if applicable. Sowilo would sound like a hissing snake, for example, while ansuz would sound like singing.

Step 3: Assess whether your object has been charged. If you can sense energy, you might feel that tingling or buzzing sensation, or you might visually see that the object continues to have a light in your mind's eye even when you're not concentrating on that visualization. Knowing when an object has been properly charged takes experience and practice, so go with your gut instinct on this one for now, and know that your ability to charge things will improve over time. Note that unlike an electrical charge, a spiritual charge can be held by an object indefinitely.

Pray with Runes and Evoke Them

The use of runes is bound to the mythology of the old gods, and it is through prayer that the manifest energy of the runes can be evoked. "Evocation" means calling upon the power that resides within the runes. Let's assume you've already charged your runes. You can think about evocation as switching them on. Many runemasters believe that the Teutonic deities are inextricably bound with the use of the runes. I personally believe that ancient mythology fuels my understanding of the runes; however, I have also personally observed prayers to deities who are not historically related to runes being answered. I've seen Christians pray to Jesus or Jehovah to evoke runes, and I pray to my Wiccan deities to evoke mine. Pray to whomever you feel comfortable, even if you're an agnostic who is using prayer as a psychological exercise to personify archetypes.

For beginners to prayer or those who are a little rusty with prayer, I recommend using a specific formula each time so that you don't accidentally forget any important components. If you're already a wiz at prayer, you can skip this instructional, but here's a mnemonic that works for me.

Adding together the first initial of each component of prayer spells out "praying": person listening, raise praise, ask for help, your deadline, imperatives for safety, note of thanks, and gracious attention. When asking for help, phrase it in a way that it sounds like it has already been manifested. The prayer begins by addressing your higher power and ends with a statement equivalent to "so be it" or "so mote it be." Prayer should always be followed by a period of listening attentively for a sign or inner answer.

Person listening: I invoke (God[s]/Goddess[es]/Spirit/Universe/my higher self/etc.).

Raise praise: You who is/are (name three positive attributes of the object of this prayer).

Ask for help: Thank you for (insert your knowing here in English or chant the names of each rune used to express the knowing).

Your deadline: (Now/by the next full moon/etc.).

Imperatives for safety: With harm to none and for the highest good of all. So may it be.

Note of thanks: In return, I offer you (worship/incense/food/drink/etc.).

Gracious attention: Blessed be.

   Meditate and then reflect on how you felt during and after.

It can be fun to chant the names of each rune that you use to write your knowing. In lieu of using a prayer format like the above, you may chant the names of each of the runes you're using in succession over and over again, like a mantra. Many advanced rune practitioners sing the names of their runes aloud like the chorus of a song. The names of the runes can sound impressive. I like chanting the foreign-sounding names of the runes because it reminds me of my childhood imaginings of witchcraft incantations, especially when accompanied by the act of drawing the runes in the air with my hands.

Offering Sacrifice and Respect

In the prayer format, I included a spiritual sacrifice as one of the important steps. When you ask for something from your higher power, it can boost your intention to give in return. I don't recommend animal sacrifice. As a vegetarian I believe in sparing the lives of animals. However, many cultures have and still do offer food or drink sacrifice by putting the offering onto a special plate reserved for the practice. The food or drink offering can be left outside for wildlife to consume as proxies for your higher power. An alternative offering is to burn sweet-smelling incense. By offering a gift, you propitiate the divine and gain favor.

Less tangible offerings to the divine can be very powerful, as long as they are connected with a sincere desire to serve spirit and to be served in return. For example, you can offer worship, song, and praise, or you can offer to give up a vice or to take up a volunteer cause. Your efforts offered in the spirit of service to the divine will be returned to you as blessings.

Sign Your Runic Object

It is good practice to sign your object in order to bind its energy to you and thus potentially prevent the misuse of your sacred tool. Many ancient runic artifacts proclaiming the name or title of the staves' carver have been found. You can sign your first name or come up with a nickname for yourself as a runemaster. Each time you carve your own name with runes, you go through the process of evoking yourself, which can be a touching spiritual experience in and of itself.

I'd love to tell you a story about discovering my spiritual name because it was a special experience for me. I was a young adult just starting college when I learned about the law of magic that states that knowing something or somebody's true name gives one power over that thing or person. Prior to this, I had thought it was a little silly that many people in my religious community had special names that they only used for ritual occasions. I joked that my name was Lady Ravensbreath Shadowcaster and refused to use anything but my given first name.

At some point, I decided that treating an important part of my religious faith tradition like a joke all the time might lead to a bit of a spiritual crisis. So I decided to pray to my gods to ask them to give me a magical name, as it is called in my Wiccan religion. I was very specific in my prayer. Magical people often say prayers like lawyers, because they know that their prayers might otherwise manifest in a myriad of unexpected ways. I asked to see my magical name in writing, rather than hear it, so that I'd know I wasn't going crazy when I got the sign.

That week, I went to the cafeteria to purchase food at my college, and outside the building I found a nametag with the name "Delriece" on it. Excited that it might be a sign, I raced to the library on campus to pick up a book about name meanings. When I opened up the name book to the page on which the name was printed, a health insurance card with another name on it fell out. My gods had given me two magical names. At the time, I decided to use the one on the name card as my public magical name at gatherings and to carve on spiritual objects that might be seen by others. The second name I kept private as a sacred name to use in spiritual exercises alone or with people I trusted like family.

You don't have to choose a magical name if you don't wish to do so, but the process of choosing a name felt like a spiritual confirmation for me and helped show me that real results are possible so that I would start to take spiritual power more seriously. Getting real results is one surefire way to get hooked on rune magic. The word "magic" in this context means that the runes create real change within you or within your world. I encourage you to experiment with your own rune spiritual exercise using the suggestions in this chapter.

five

Specific Applications of Runes

I've created a small collection of rune applications that are inspired by ancient mythological applications of the runes, many of which are still applicable today. Read through the examples and try them out using the rune rules we just learned. When you see rune magic in action, you will believe in the power of your runes. You can also use the examples as a template to perform your own related spiritual exercises in order to tailor your results to the desires in your own heart.

To Protect and Give Strength
to a Traveler for a Safe Journey

In olden times, travelers often carried a walking staff in order to blaze trails through the wilderness, to climb hills and mountains, and to use as a weapon against unsavory characters or vicious animals found along their paths. Making a runestaff is popular because runes are tied to staffs in several ways. The word "stave" means "staff" and is also the word we use for the rune symbols that we carve. You know that several of the runes are associated with tree woods such as yew (eihwaz) and birch (berkanan). Trees are more than just a crafting material. A runestaff represents a branch of the mythological world tree that is the universe. Your runestaff can act as a magic wand, directing spiritual energy out into the world to create what you desire.

Choose a runestaff based on the type of wood you have available. I've made runestaffs out of many types of wood collected as fallen wood or mindfully cut from trees, but I also made one out of a pine dowel purchased from a lumber store that worked just fine. Traditional runestaffs matched the height of the user or were sometimes even taller than a person, but I've also made smaller ones. My favorite traveling staff is the size of a short cane, so I can easily bring it on an airplane as a carry-on item.

Luckily for us, it is easy to fit positive traveling wishes into a single rune. Beginners may find single rune exercises much easier than carving a huge line of runes. Recall that brevity is actually an asset that advanced runemasters seek to attain. I recommend jera from the Elder Futhark for a travel staff if you're looking for a positive journey. You might wish to substitute or add raido, if speed is important to your travels, or ansuz, if you feel that your mode of travel or destination might be very dangerous.

You can carve your rune stave proudly near the top of your runestaff and face it forward when you walk so that its power clears your path. If you feel the need to be discreet with your use of runes, you can carve the rune on the bottom of your staff. You can leave your staff with a wooden base because it looks neat to make rune prints when walking on the beach or in mud. If you want to protect your runestaff from damage, you can carve the rune on the bottom and then cover it with a rubber base that you can purchase from the hardware store.

To Calm Sea Waves

Traveling over calm waters was of great concern to ancient seafaring people. Even today, drowning and boating accidents are ever-present dangers for those who venture out on open water. Waves are also metaphors for emotions. Even if you never so much as go near a swimming pool, you may have use for calming the inner tides of your emotions. This is another single-rune exercise, but take your time choosing the right place and time to charge the rune. As experienced as I am with the runes and with meditation, the feeling of peacefulness is one of the most difficult emotions to conjure up at will for me. Don't perform this exercise when you're feeling stressed out, rushed, angry, or any other kind of emotional turmoil. The exercise to calm metaphorical and literal sea waves is necessarily performed outdoors, so you'll also need to choose a time when the winds are still.

Procure a blue ribbon with length equal to the circumference of your head to symbolically contain the emotions you'll be calming, and find a red pen. The color blue is to represent peace, and the red of the pen is merely traditional to activation of the runes. For practical reasons, cutting runes into a ribbon is not necessary. Wait until a time when the winds and your own inner feelings are at peace. Go to a peaceful outdoor location, perhaps by a calm lake or in a garden. Seat yourself comfortably, close your eyes and breathe slowly and deeply. Let go of any lingering worries about your day and allow thoughts of the external world at large to drift away. Notice when your breathing naturally slows and your muscles begin to relax.

When you feel ready, write laguz nine times on one side of the ribbon, spacing the staves apart equally. Nine is a number of success and completion, peace and joy. Keep the ribbon in a bag or pocket to touch, or tie it anywhere you like for when you need calming energy.

To Break a Curse

Hex-Breaking Rune Wheel

If you believe that a curse has been placed upon you, go to a three-way crossroads and draw this design with a handful of graveyard dirt. Walk away without looking back. You will leave the curse at that crossroads to harmlessly recede into the earth. This particular hex-breaking rune wheel is made up of ken, thurisaz, and uruz, which together give the imagery of the transformative power of lightning and a rainstorm running its course, saying, "Light blasts away evil. This force is overpowered."

To Control the Weather

Here's how to make a cloud-busting magic wand or a wand that will otherwise help you control the weather. Note that controlling the weather, though an old practice, is not without its ethical conundrums. If you change the weather, many other people might be affected, and even local weather changes might possibly affect global weather systems. Some believe that temperamental entities whose domain is weather might become mischievous or malevolent toward those who work weather magic. If you choose to attempt to control the weather, I advise that you do so only with great care and consideration as well as prayers that it not bring harm to anyone or anything. That said, the information on how to make a weather wand is below for educational purposes.

Making a rune wand is very much like making a rune-staff, so refer to the earlier exercise for information on choosing wood. In my religious tradition, a wand is typically the same as the length between one's elbow and fingertips. Some curious local weather lore in my region claims that a whistle made from horsetail will call the winds. You can use a horsetail whistle as a wand or choose a type of wood that is sacred and practical to you. Carefully carve the rune wheel around the wand (it should wrap around much like a circular sticker), but remember to carve the runes in order.

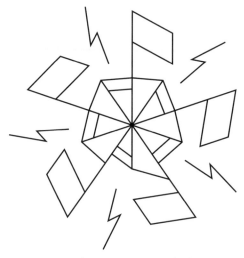

Weather Magic Rune Wheel

This spiritual exercise makes use of a rune wheel of ansuz, uruz, hagalaz, and sowilo, carved in that order. The knowing for this rune wheel and the weather wand created by it is this: "Advisor of rain, hail, and sunshine blessings." Observe that every instance of the rainy energy of uruz and destructive weather power of hagalaz is counterbalanced by touching both the divine guidance of ansuz and the sunshine of sowilo. Remember to read the staves in order, from the center of the rune wheel outward, whenever you look upon the wheel. Notice, also, that isa can be seen throughout the wheel. Of course, it's easy to see a straight line anywhere, but it is particularly meaningful that the rune representing ice should be here to stop the natural weather in the path of what it was doing to follow your own advisement.

To Ward Off Evil Influences

Here's a simple exercise that makes use of a bindrune to ward off specific evil influences. I encourage you to invent your own bindrune using ansuz and a rune that is specific to any danger that you fear. As an example, I've combined ansuz with thurisaz. Ansuz offers stable and friendly protection while thurisaz, just as the thorn protects the rose, offers protective influence as well as represents the danger from which you should be protected.

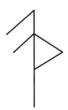

Bindrune to Ward Off Evil

For this spiritual exercise, I'll ask that you depart from the ordinary rune rules by not cutting this bindrune, since the suggested use is for placement on the back of your hand. Even if you're game for cutting yourself, it would likely ruin the energy of this particular spiritual work because of the pain and harm inflicted. The back-of-the-hand placement is visible, if you want it to be, and represents a protective slap to your enemies. Instead, I suggest that you write this bindrune in red or black ink on the back of your hand. If you're not shy about displaying staves, write the bindrune in permanent ink. If you want to keep your protective magic hidden, write the bindrune in washable marker and then wash it off after your prayers and offerings. Washing off ink is a secrecy technique used by witches that works quite well for me.

For Invisibility

This bindrune doesn't actually make somebody invisible, but rather it coats whatever bears this sign with the energy that tells surrounding viewers "this is somebody else's problem." I have used this rune on private diaries so that should somebody happen across them, they wouldn't bother to pick them up and read them. You can certainly wear this bindrune as an emblem if you want to go unnoticed. For example, you might use it if you want to be left alone at your workplace to get your work done instead of being constantly bothered by well-meaning coworkers. However, always be mindful if you choose to carry this bindrune on your person, lest you be ignored in an emergency. Never carry this bindrune in a car. Sure, a police officer may not notice you speeding, but you might be hit by a car whose driver did not notice you either.

The bindrune for invisibity, or "somebody else's problem," is a combination of mannaz, neid, pertho, and tiwaz. The runes allow for the element of chance to cause the bindrune to be passed by for more important things. Write the rune with a pen on any object you'd like to keep private. It's okay to omit the carving of this bindrune, but please make sure to charge the runes so that you are directing this powerful energy away from yourself and onto the symbol.

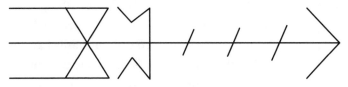

Invisibility Bindrune

Remember that in some cases you may think you need invisibility, but what you actually need is protection. When I was in high school, I tried to make myself invisible because I wanted to avoid the eyes of bullies who happened to be teachers. Certainly my magic worked. I was safely ignored by the teachers who had previously seemed out to get me. However, I also wasn't getting the help that I needed in the subjects with which I was struggling. I also had an impossible time making friends in high school and couldn't even spend time with my friends while at school. I felt isolated and spent my high school years playing catch-up with friends outside of school. What I could have used more than invisibility was some protection and empowerment. What I'm trying to say is that you shouldn't use powers of invisibility to avoid problems that can be solved by communication.

To Blunt Swords or Otherwise Calm Confrontations in Your Favor

Runes are known for having the power to dull the blades of enemy weapons. I've never been in a sword fight, so I haven't had the opportunity to test this. However, blunting swords can also be a metaphor for tipping the odds of the outcome of a confrontation in your favor while not directly influencing the will of another person. For many modern practitioners who use runes to create spiritual change, it feels ethically wrong to directly change the mind or emotions of another person. Some believe that this forced removal of control can easily backfire or otherwise cause the person who is doing the coercion to experience similar negative effects in his or her own life as a reflection of what has been projected into the universe. A magical law of attraction states that spiritual energy attracts more of its same character as you work with it, so using controlling energy will draw more controlling people and situational factors into your own life. Undertake such spiritual work with caution and deliberate over it in prayer.

Blunting Bindrune

The ethical gray area of gently inclining your opponent to change his or her mind or tactics by affecting the environment or situation is addressed in this exercise. A suggested bindrune for the knowing "Blunt my opponent's sword" is to cross two tiwaz staves, representing conflict, and top them with the peaceful, protective energy of laguz to bring love and emotional reconsideration into play. Note that unless you actually carve these runes into a weapon of your enemy, using and empowering these runes will also cause you to be more peaceful in the conflict. I hope that this exercise will help you consider that when you use runes, you are changing your inner self just as much as your external world.

To Draw Love

Writing down what you want is a wonderful way to clarify your needs, regardless of whether you use runes to do the writing. My mother told me about how she wrote down the aspects of a husband that she wanted, and like magic that man appeared in her life. She believed that she may have inadvertently caused a spiritual miracle to happen by the simple act of writing down what she wanted. Her husband fit each and every characteristic on her list for a perfect mate. She certainly didn't conjure him into existence, nor did she force him to love her with a magic spell. Instead, by focusing her energy on her needs, she painted a big cosmic target on herself to draw people who had those characteristics into her life or perhaps to help her notice where they were in the world all around her.

Just as it is thought by many spiritual practitioners to be improper to force your enemies to lay down their weapons directly, it is also ethically tricky to perform love magic in any form. Forcing somebody to love you takes away their willpower and the chance for that person to discover how to love someone all on his or her own. Love magic can also backfire easily into obsessions or even hatred. As a fortune-teller, I understand that many of my clients desire the love of a certain unobtainable person. Often it's an ex-boyfriend or ex-girlfriend, but generally an ex is an ex for good reason. As a teenager, I was also desperate for crushes to return my affections. Luckily for me at the time, a friend suggested the idea of generally drawing love into my life rather than targeting a specific person. The spiritual benefits of drawing love not only allow a person to achieve the goal of being in a loving relationship, but this can also have good side effects of making a person more lovable and generally creating love and harmony in families and friendships that surround the person.

This application makes use of the runic practice of writing on objects in something other than straight lines from left to right. People who used the runes as a script often wrote up and down or layered lines first going in one direction, say left to right, and then the other, from right to left. Runes sometimes march around gravestones or other monuments to form pretty designs. In the case of this exercise you will be writing the runes in the design of a spiral that first winds from the center outward and then turns and winds inward like a labyrinth.

The act of writing a repeated mantra or knowing is something that is practiced in many religious traditions. In this exercise we'll depart again from the tradition of cutting the runes because, for a beginner, this volume of rune work is best done with pen and paper. You'll need a circular piece of white paper and a red pen. It's okay to cut a regular piece of printer paper into a circle, but the bigger the piece of paper, the more valuable this meditative act becomes because it will take more of your time.

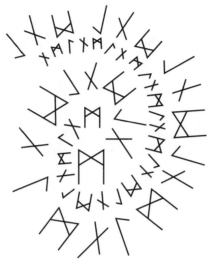

To Draw Love

Beginning at the very center of the piece of paper, begin writing this sequence of runes: mannaz, neid, laguz. The
knowing for this is "I need love." Technically, it means "Hu-
mankind needs love," but in this case mannaz represents you.
If you have a personal rune, bindrune, or other sigil, you may
use it instead if you prefer. Write the rune sequence over and
over again and without spaces or punctuation. As you write,
curve your line and turn the paper so that the sequence winds
in an increasing spiral counterclockwise on the page. Leave a
large gap between the arm and the outer ring so that you can
fit the row back in when you reach the edge of the page. When
you do reach the edge of the page, change your stave order to
laguz, neid, mannaz as you spiral back inward. The knowing

has changed to "Love needs me." Place the completed piece of paper under a pillow inside its pillowcase. When you begin to see the results of love being drawn into your life, burn the paper as an offering and know that the effects will then be intensified by the transformative power of the flames.

To Talk with Birds

When I was a child, my mother told me the bit of folklore that if you sprinkle salt on a bird's tail, it will be yours. I'm sure the idea behind it is that birds might be easier to catch if their tails, used as rudders for flight, were somehow disabled with heaps of salt. But in my child mind, the saltshaker became a magic tool that would make the bird love me forever. I spent hours sneaking up on birds to sprinkle salt on their tails, coming so close to them that I could have easily just caught one with one of my butterfly nets. I never did capture a bird using salt alone, and salt did not hamper their flight in the slightest nor make them want to be my friends despite my having salted many confused and unsuspecting birds quite thoroughly.

Runes, too, are legendary bird-taming tools. If you view this myth as yet another metaphor, the bird itself is a symbolic messenger. The spiritual exercise To Talk with Birds is a knowing for being able to communicate clearly and effectively even across long distances. Putting clear intention into runes in order to communicate your message is a wonderful way to galvanize yourself toward presenting your message in the best possible way. You can use this exercise when you are going to apply for jobs, if you're hoping to get a call on the telephone from a long-lost love or estranged family member, or if you're writing a book.

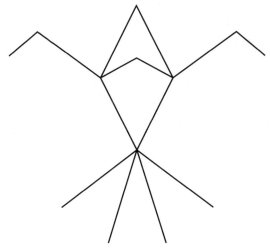

To Talk with Birds

For this exercise, you'll need to procure a feather from a bird, preferably the tail feather. You can use a feather from a pet bird, a found feather from a wild one, or even a feather from a craft store if necessary. You'll also need a palmful of salt. Go outside to a place with bare dirt, sand, or dust. Carve the bindrune of ken for communication and eihwaz to represent the flight of birds (or your messages that you want communicated) as arrows from a yew bow; note that the bindrune looks like a bird. Carve the bindrune in the dirt with the pinky finger of your dominant hand.

Next, read the bindrune and lay the feather vertically across the bindrune in the dirt. Seal the feather into the bindrune by lightly sprinkling salt to paint the lines of your rune with it. As you work with this bindrune, clearly visualize your message getting through to the right people in the right place and at the right time, allowing yourself to feel the emotions you would feel if you were to successfully communicate your message. You'll be leaving your bindrune where you carved it, so for this reason it's important not to use so much salt that you'll make the dirt inhospitable to plant or animal life that might take hold there.

You can use this bindrune, or others you create yourself, for communication in other ways as well. I have many friends who hide runes on their websites in order to enhance the message of the website. One way to do this is to open up an art program to create an image the size of one of the pictures on your website. Draw the stave with the program's pen tool and then paste the ordinary site picture on top of the charged bindrune. Save the image as the latest version, and you now have an empowered image file with a hidden rune that you can display on your website to enhance its effectiveness.

To Soothe Sorrows

When grief or sorrow hits me, I turn to spirituality to keep me levelheaded. Runes can be a great comfort, consoling one with a sense of empowerment and something to do spiritually in situations when one might be otherwise helpless. When my dad died, I'd turn to my husband and tell him that I needed to go pray. I'd spend hours in prayer, devastated that all of the healing magical work I had done for him had ultimately failed. It was only when I turned to combat my own sorrows instead of beating myself up that I was able to think clearly about the role rune magic can play in the spirituality of life and death transitions.

I now believe that runes can help keep somebody alive just like a respirator in a hospital can help somebody cling to life, but those interventions are not always the best nor what the person chooses through his or her own force of will. Sometimes, all you can offer loved ones who are going through a problem is your own love and positive energy, leaving the rest to them and the universe. A favorite spiritual poet of mine named Gwen Thompson wrote a mysterious knowing for sorrow that helped me conceptualize this spiritual exercise: "When misfortune is enow, wear the blue star on thy brow."

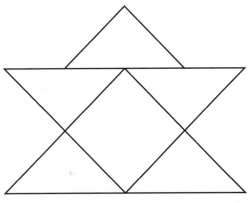

To Soothe Sorrows

If you want to carve the runes, you can make yourself a metal headband out of a length of bendable metal, scratch the runes on the headband, and paint the runes with blue paint. A simpler way to perform this exercise is to use makeup to draw the lines on your forehead temporarily and then wipe them off after you decide you're done wearing the bindrune. You can leave it on for the day or an evening or wipe it off as soon as you're done creating it, while remembering the mark in your mind's eye whenever you look in the mirror until your sorrows abate. The bindrune I suggest is a combination of two wunjo staves upside down and facing one another but with their tails together, a berkanan stave with points down, and a ken stave topping off the star. From bottom to top they represent divine joy coming from sorrow through nurturing love and rising up like a fire from within. When read from the top down, they can represent the fires of divine love nurturing joy through you here on earth. The star that they form works as another sigil, meaning protection from misfortune, to add power to the runes. As you draw the bindrune, concentrate on your own divine source of spiritual inner strength.

To Heal

Runes can be used for healing in so very many ways, and many combinations of runes can be used to heal as well. I advise you to experiment with your own bindrunes and runic alphabets that you associate with healing and to try different techniques of applying runes to objects for the person in need of healing. Runes can be carved on the stems of flowers brought to someone in the hospital, drawn in the air over medications with a fingertip, or even knitted into a blanket. Again, there are many rune combinations that can be used and I encourage you to discover your own. I like to make a little rune wheel from fehu and dagaz because it reminds me of a little healing chant in Spanish that my daughter taught me that, roughly translated, says, "Heal, heal. If you are not better today, you will be tomorrow."

I like to use rune wheels for healing, imagining that I'm painting a target for healing. Some people believe that healing is an energy that can be bestowed upon a person from the divine, and some people believe that healing comes from within. The visual inward and outward design of a rune wheel can evoke thoughts of both or either of these processes depending on what works for you. This rune wheel has four radiating spokes.

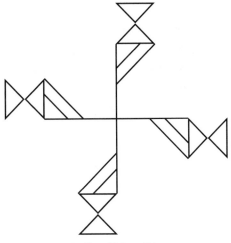

Healing Helm of Awe

I have two suggested applications for this helm of awe. If you are asking for healing, go to a tree, preferably a birch tree (representing the nurturing force of berkanan), and carve the helm of awe on the bark on the south side of the tree, which receives the most of the sun's healing rays. When you pray, consider asking the tree to act as the world tree and deliver the healing that is in the universe to its rightful place. The connection between Mother Earth and Father Sky here will aid in natural healing for whomever needs it.

For those who are healthcare providers or those who want to be healers, I have yet another application of these runes. Scratch a simpler healing bindrune on the fingernail of your ring finger, and then paint over it with fingernail polish. I suggest using a tool that is not too sharp to do the scratching, such as a bent paperclip. You don't want to injure yourself; just scratch the nail surface a tiny bit. If you want to use the runes as a decorative nail design, it's okay to paint the bindrune on all of your nails. Conversely, if you want to hide the rune, you may use washable ink instead of nail polish, wash it off, and then brush the etched rune with clear or any color nail polish or cuticle oil to hide its presence.

Healing Bindrune

To Still the Senses

As the mother to two preschoolers, I have my work cut out for me when it comes to keeping calm in a chaotic environment. My house is loud and messy, and sometimes a child's tantrum leads me to have an immature tantrum of my own. It takes all of my willpower to reign in my anger or disappointment in order to attempt to teach my children to be civilized people. Sometimes, I just plain lose my cool.

A vital skill for anyone who works with runes is the ability to clear one's mind and inner emotional landscape in order to allow the feelings and energy of each rune to channel through. I definitely understand that sitting even for a few long seconds in quiet meditation is a challenge for the beginner. I struggled to master meditation all throughout my teenage years with little success. Even though I was convinced that meditating for only five minutes was a pitiful attempt, it was the most that I could do on a good day. In hindsight, I realize now that five minutes of meditation can be an achievement for anyone. Using runes to help you calm and center yourself can help you become a better meditator and can increase the effectiveness of all spiritual exercises you perform with the runes.

For this spiritual exercise, you'll need some dry, powdered turmeric, which is an herb associated with healing, mental peace, and spirituality. You can find turmeric in the spice or bulk section of your grocery store. Mix the turmeric with skin-safe red powder such as kumkum powder, usually available in an Indian grocery store, or red powdered rouge or eye shadow. You'll be making a batch of magic powder that you can use on many occasions. For your first batch, you can make a small batch using only a quarter cup of each if you like. When you wish to still your senses and become more peaceful, mix a tiny bit of the powder with olive oil and apply it to your forehead between the eyes.

To Enhance Memory, Speech, and Mental Acuity

I'm a scatterbrained, distractible person. When I was a child and later as an adult, medical professionals diagnosed my awesome multitasking skill as attention-deficit/hyperactivity disorder, but I like to think of my flighty Gemini brain as a strength. Thinking quickly and connecting many related thoughts makes me a better teacher because I can't possibly ramble on about one subject long enough for my students to become bored. Using the power of the runes to enhance concentration, however, can aid my writing and my vocation as a mother considerably. I can't tell you how many minutes of my life I spend standing in front of the pantry, wondering what ingredient or food I was about to choose.

I like a useful spiritual exercise with runes to produce an equally practical runic object. Here are some simple instructions for making a runic talisman. You can make talismans for any purpose you like, but I think that having one handy to wear as a pendant whenever I need extra brain help is wonderful. I have a number of runic talismans for various purposes hanging in my closet. Whenever I need the help of runes for a specific challenge coming up that day, I can grab a talisman before I head out the door in the morning.

I believe for several reasons that the best runic talismans are those made from wood. First, you can perform all the runic procedures necessary, including carving. Second, the associations of runes with wood and with the world tree increase the power of the spiritual exercise. Third, a carefully sanded rune talisman feels good against the skin when worn as a pendant. It's comforting to handle my talisman until it is well oiled with my own skin oils. Finally, the technique for making a wooden talisman is identical to the one in chapter 6 for making runes. You can just add a drilled hole or a fastener to suspend it from a strap or chain. In fact, when making runes, you can save the end pieces off the branch you're using to cut the runes for future talismans. My suggested runes for memory, speech, and enhancing your mental strengths are mannaz, ansuz, and sowilo. Note that ingwaz forms in the center between the two mannaz symbols, initiating the energy whenever you look at the image.

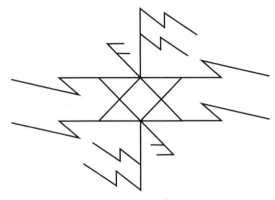

To Enhance Memory, Speech, and Mental Acuity

Luck and Winning at Games

I believe the runes are lucky, and I love to make them into good luck charms for specific purposes. For luck with money I can slip a piece of paper with a rune upon it in my wallet. For good luck while driving to keep me clear of heavy traffic and accidents, I can quickly trace a rune on my dashboard. The rune pertho speaks specifically to games of chance, since some runeologists believe its stave represents a dice cup. For this spiritual exercise, I'm going to combine the runes with common folklore regarding luck. Using runes may not help you win the lottery, but everyone could use a little more luck in this game of chance we call life.

For this spiritual exercise, you'll need a coin. This activity is best performed on a Sunday, since Sunday is generally associated with success. You will cut or scratch pertho onto the coin. If you are going to be playing a game of chance with dice, rub the coin on the dice before throwing. Instead of painting the rune on the coin alone, paint it also onto the bottoms of your feet, so that luck may walk with you wherever you go. Take the coin outside and throw it to the ground, stepping upon it until it is compressed into the dirt. If practical, use your bare feet to stomp on the coin so that the runes painted on your foot will contact the coin. Without looking, reach down to pick the coin back up, put it in your pocket, and walk away without looking back. Carry the coin with you as a charm. If you do win money with your lucky charm, donate a portion of your winnings to the poor as an offering of thanks.

To Protect a Home from Bad Luck or Intruders

It's possible that the angular construction and exterior decoration of some Germanic peoples' homes may have hidden runes in plain sight. It is an old practice in many cultures to curse potential home invaders with a protective charm before any break-in occurs. Recall that some spiritual teachers believe that any negative energy can reflect back on you if you use it. However, since the practice of using negativity to ward away negativity is a tried and true one in many cultures, I will show an example here. If you'd like to avoid using negativity, you can substitute algiz for the following bindrune.

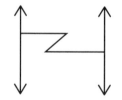

Home Defense Bindrune

The bindrune indicated here is a combination of sowilo, hagalaz, and tiwaz. Combined they are a powerful sigil for the knowing "Power given to the justice that destroys enemies." Place this rune on a material of your choice and then apply it to the hearth of your home. You can place it on a fireplace mantle or hang it above the fireplace like a holiday stocking. If you don't have a hearth, place the rune in your kitchen. Before central heating and electric stoves, the hearth was the heart and life of a home and was where all heating and cooking took place. Another potential placement for this rune is carved on the doorframe or threshold.

To Commemorate the Dead

We have plenty of archeological evidence that runes have been historically written on grave markers. Runes are a wonderful way to connect with spirits or memories of those who have passed on because they represent the stories, ideas, and experiences we've shared in this lifetime. Of course, you may not have the liberty or ability to painstakingly chisel runes on the grave markers of your ancestors or friends. To commemorate the dead, I often turn to the simple cross-cultural act of raising a toast to a deceased loved one.

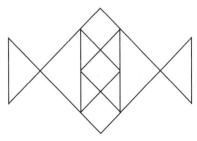

Ancestor-Honoring Bindrune

To commemorate a deceased loved one with a toast, you'll need a cup and a beverage of your choice. You can use a wooden cup in order to permanently carve the runes, or just trace them with a finger in the condensation on a glass that you've stored in the freezer for this purpose. Inside the cup along the rim, write out the name of the deceased person in runes. Use the beverage to exactly trace the letters that you already wrote so that you're writing each rune twice to imitate the actions of both carving and then painting the runes. Remember that you'll be spelling his or her name phonetically and without using any spaces. If you don't have a specific person in mind or don't know the name of the deceased, I suggest you use a phrase such as "To my ancestors, known and unknown." The named and unnamed dead can be represented by othila and dagaz. My bindrune design is meant to evoke the mythology of birth, love, death, and rebirth while still being simple enough to carve or trace on a cup.

How to Sneak Success Runes into the Workplace and Other Useful Tricks

Being able to choose your own workplace decor is a freedom that I encourage you to express. You can bring runes and other meaningful symbols into play in your work. When I was a kid, my parents owned their own business. I made a fehu sigil for my mom, and she placed it by her computer to encourage the financial success of the business. Since fortune-telling is what I do, I can be overt about placing runes and other symbols all over my working space if I like. Runes don't have to be outwardly occult looking, though, in order to be effective.

You can certainly sneak fehu under your keyboard or secret it away in your purse or day planner. Since the runes are such aesthetically pleasing angular designs, you can also hide them in plain sight. Notice how the rune fehu repeated can become a border for a picture frame or for stationary. As you've seen from the examples of bindrunes in this book, there are many ways to combine runes to further obscure their meanings for others while simultaneously enhancing their meanings for yourself. If curious coworkers searched for images of runes on the Internet, they wouldn't necessarily be able to spot a bindrune. Unless, of course, they were already very familiar with the runes and thus sympathetic to their use.

Fehu Border Example

six

Making Runes Your Personalized Divination System

When I was a child, I was obsessed with secret codes and languages. I had an Egyptian hieroglyphics rubber stamp set that I would use to fill sheets of paper with prose. I memorized Morse code and spent hours with a flashlight sending signals to friends in the dark. I gravitated toward storybooks that included special alphabets like the Dinotopia series by James Gurney. For one birthday party, I made up my own cryptic alphabet and my parents printed out small cheat sheets for all of the kids so that they could decode clues for a treasure hunt. Imagine my delight when, as an adult, I learned that plenty of grownups are inventing their own special alphabets to learn more about themselves, keep private things private, and tell fortunes with new divination systems.

How to Buy Runes

It is good luck to receive a set of runes as a gift. Rune sets can be purchased on the Internet or in metaphysical bookstores. The most common set of runes available are the Elder Futhark runes. If you don't know which type of runes to choose, the Elder Futhark is a good place to start. It'll be familiar to other rune aficionados, should you run into any, and if you read further advanced literature about runes, it's likely to be included.

Some prefer to choose divination tools in-person, rather than buying them online or waiting for them to be provided as a gift. The theory behind this is that the essence or energy of the runes can be sensed through the hands or other sensory perceptions. To use this method of choosing runes, go to a metaphysical bookstore that supplies runes and run your hands over the available sets of runes. You may sense the set that is best for you as warmth, coolness, a prickling sensation, a fuzziness, or simply an internal thought that they feel right. In some belief systems, it is unlucky to haggle for a tool like this, so consider paying the sticker price even if bargaining is something you normally do.

How to Make Runes

To make your own set of runes, you'll need to first choose the base material upon which to mark the runes. This may depend on what runes you choose. The largest runic alphabet is the Anglo-Saxon runes with thirty-three characters, to which some people add one blank rune. The smallest runic system is the Witch's Runes, which number thirteen. Obviously, you don't want to choose hunks of gold for your runes, or you'll go broke. Again, if you don't know which runic alphabet to choose, select the Elder Futhark, for which you'll need twenty-five rune bases if you include the optional blank rune. Your base materials should also be all roughly the same size and shape. As you get used to your runes, you don't want to inadvertently begin identifying the runes by feel as you select them. Keep the rune selection process during divination as random as possible by not allowing the base shapes of the runes to give them away as your hand grabs for them.

Runes can be made of clay, stone, wood, deer antler, bone, ceramic tiles, crystals, resin, fruit pits, and more. Consider affordability and durability when choosing your runes. My first runes were made with stones I found outside my home and a permanent marker, which I don't recommend because the oils in your skin will rub the markings off over time. Likewise, paints are likely to chip from the runes tumbling against one another. The most durable runes are those with markings carved or etched into their bases.

Runes of stone are the most popular modern type, even though ancient runes were most likely made of wood. You can purchase polished rocks, leave your rocks natural, or use a rock tumbler to polish your own. You can also look up the associations for common semiprecious gemstones on the Internet. For example, amethyst stones correspond well with healing runes. You'll also need a rotary tool with a cutting or engraving bit. In addition, you may want to buy waterproof paint or a permanent marker to fill the etched markings in. This will make them pop. A thicker paint will make the runes smoother to the touch, thereby enhancing random selection. Carve the markings into the stones, one per stone, and leave one optional blank rune. Carefully fill the etchings with contrasting paint, if you like, and wait for them to dry completely before use. The paint can be whatever color you choose. I don't use plastic sealant on my runes because, for me, touching the stone, bone, wood or other material is an important component of getting in the right headspace.

Ancient runes may have been painted with red paint. You can even paint your runes with your own blood if you're not squeamish, but take care to keep your runes to yourself and to wash your hands and workspace when finished using them. You can make staves in whatever single color shows itself best on the stones or other bases you've chosen, or you can pick multiple colors that help you remember the meanings. Whatever color you associate with the meanings is best. For example, for a rune that means war, I chose red because I associated it with blood-red imagery. Here are some more color associations that work for me, but please choose your own associations over mine if they conflict. Keep in mind that the rocks you choose may have color that can enhance the meaningfulness for you as well.

Red: War, conflict, passion, sex, violence, hearth or flame. Fehu, thurisaz, raido, ken, tiwaz, mannaz.
Pink: Love, femininity, family.
Orange: Success, victory, energy, masculinity.
Yellow: Intellect, travel by air, study. Wunjo, sowilo, ingwaz, othila.

Green: Money, fertility, growth and change, travel over land, gifts, birth, wealth. Uruz, berkanan.

Blue: Healing, sadness, travel by water, justice, sea. Hagalaz, jera, dagaz, ansuz, gebo, eihwaz, laguz.

Purple: Spirituality, femininity, joy, destiny.

Brown: Nature, earth, animals, stagnation.

Black: Protection, balance, hiding. Neid, isa, pertho.

White: Spirituality, healing, protection, stagnation, balance.

Silver: Divine feminine. Ehwaz.

Gold: Divine masculine.

Gray: War, Tyr.

A set of black runes with red letters that is reserved for only speaking with the dead can be made from any material. I suggest using a dark or stained wood or black polymer clay, but you can also use glazed clay, black stones, or whatever you like. The practice of casting black runes to talk to spirits was taught by the goddess Freya, who instructed the gods on how to conduct a "sitting out" (a type of séance).

Runes of polymer clay are easy to make if you have an oven. Polymer clay can be purchased at a craft store, shaped, and then carved or imprinted with rune symbols. When choosing the uniform shape for all your rune bases, it's best to have runes that lie flat with the runic symbol on top or on the bottom. So, think of something flat with two sides, like a poker chip or a domino. Whether they have rounded edges or pointed edges is up to your preference, as is the size. Select for visibility. I like runes big enough that I can read them when I cast them on the ground even if I'm standing up, but it's nice to have smaller runes that fit into a purse for travel as well.

I'd also like to extoll the virtues of wooden runes. Ash and elm are represented in Norse mythology, along with many other woods. The rowan tree is the "tree of runes" and its wood is well known for its innate protection magic. Oak is also a popular choice due to its toughness and because it is sacred to the god Thor, but prepare for a lot of work if you want to hand carve your staves in hardwood. You can buy wooden pieces or cut your own and then burn them with a wood-burning pen, available in most craft stores. I find that wood burning is much easier, but some believe that cutting the staves while singing the runic sounds is a magical act in and of itself. I use a utility knife with a replaceable blade, available in hardware stores, and bend the tip of the blade with pliers to form a groove to scoop out tiny bits of wood to make the staves.

Ritual for Harvesting Wood for Runes

Fallen wood can be used for runes if you can find a piece that is about two feet (sixty centimeters) long and one to two inches (two to five centimeters) in diameter. You'll slice this into quarter-inch (five-millimeter) rounds later and sand them smooth. The only tree that is unlucky to cut or burn for runes would be the elder tree, because it is sacred to the Elder Mother Goddess of Wicca. Other trees are fine to harvest from, but you may observe these ritual steps in order to imbue your runes with respect for the divine.

Step 1: Select an offering to give to the tree spirits in exchange for the wood. Traditional offerings are ale or other alcohol for the gods or milk and sweets for the fairies. A pragmatic modern offering to the tree is compost and water.

Bring the offering, a hand saw, and a black ribbon with you when you go to harvest.

Step 2: Find a place to harvest wood, and make sure that you have permission to take the wood from the owners of the property and the tree.

Step 3: Gain permission from the tree spirit by knocking thrice on the tree and talking to it. Explain the intent of your rune making and give the offering to the base of the tree. Ask the tree for permission to take its wood and then wait in silence and listen for any negative omens for a few moments. If all feels well, knock on the branch you are going to cut to encourage the tree spirits to flee into the trunk of the tree, and then tie the black ribbon around the branch on the tree side of where you're going to cut. Think of it like an energetic tourniquet.

Step 4: Cut the branch swiftly. Give thanks to the tree. Untie the ribbon and save for future use only for this purpose. You may choose to rub mud onto the tree's "wound" as a healing balm for it if practical. Then take your leave. It's okay if forest creatures nibble on the cakes or other offerings as proxies for the tree spirits. Finish the wooden runes however you like or leave them natural. This is an affordable, durable, and lightweight option.

Other Options

A script similar to runes, the ogham is traditionally marked on sticks that can then be cast or drawn at random as if you were drawing straws.

Similar to wood, fruit pits such as peach pits or avocado pits can be carved. Eat a delicious avocado and then split the pit in half with a pocketknife along the natural seam. Each pit can make two runes. They can be carved easily, like potatoes, when fresh. They dry hard and can be sanded and treated with oil or other finishers as you wish.

As a child, I wore a rune of protection carved from bone and painted black as a pendant. A rune set made from bones is a nod toward the probable precursor of rune divination—the act of casting bones or stones and divining the future from the patterns in which they lie. With the powerful symbolism of life and death, animal bones seem to possess a special energy. Since I'm a vegetarian, I don't always have ready access to animal bones, but I always pick up dried bones when I find them on the ground in order to construct rune sets. A hike in old farmlands or desert areas can yield plenty of old bones. These can be carefully carved with a knife or rotary tool and coated with polymer to preserve them if you wish. Be careful with bone rune sets, as they are fragile. Avoid divination methods that involve casting them on a hard surface. Reserve them for meditation or gently drawing them one at a time out of a bag, or cast them only on thick cloth or soft sand.

Storing and Protecting Your Runes

Don't forget the bag! It is not an optional part of rune divination. A bag in which to keep your runes is an important part of the divination system, as one way of using runes is to simply mix them up while they're still concealed within the bag and draw one rune at random. A black cloth bag is also sometimes thought to protect and preserve runes from external energy that might affect their readings. Choose or make your own cloth bag that is thin enough that you can gently roll the runes through the cloth in your hands to mix them up for random drawing. A black velvet drawstring pouch is a common and ideal bag for runes. However, if you prefer, you can choose other colors and decorate your bag however you wish. It's best to get a new bag for your runes rather than repurpose an old one because the energies of the used bag are thought to affect the runes.

In between readings, store your runes in the bag. Some people choose to expose their runes to moonlight during the full moon or to sunlight by placing them on a windowsill or outdoors. This is done in order to charge the runes with energy for success by the sunlight and with energies that help intuition with the moonlight. If you choose to lay out your rune stones to collect moon energy, return them to the bag afterward in order to preserve the purity of the lunar energy. The bag itself will seem to take on a life of its own after a time, having bonded with its contents, and it may seem strange to put a different set of runes in that bag.

You may also wish to have a cloth onto which you can cast your runes. This tool is vital if you are using breakable runes made of particularly fragile stones, bones, or clay. If you toss your runes on a cement floor and they break, it will be very distressing, not to mention a rather bad omen of the potentials of the runes you broke being unexpressed. Avoid this tragedy by treating breakable runes gently and using a thick cloth onto which you can gently lay or cast your runes. Traditional casting cloths may have been white in color, according to Tacitus, and so it is used in modern times as well. Having a casting cloth is an excellent tool for a beginner, too, since you can mark casting cloths with your favorite rune-casting charts or spreads.

It's worth noting that some people choose to never let others handle their runes, in order to keep their energies purely personal. This is also a good practical step to take if you painted your runes with real blood, as some blood-borne pathogens are known to stay viable in dried blood for up to ten days, and other contaminates could remain virulent even longer. Therefore, if you run into other rune aficionados, it's important to ask permission before touching their runes. I keep sets of runes that are safe for others to handle and welcome my clients to cast them for me if they wish.

Getting Creative with Runic Divination

We have our own personal connections to the runes, but what each one means is well established in history. We come up with our own interpretations and ways to understand the main meaning. Each rune has a specific meaning, and the meanings don't change. But even as a beginner, you can be inspired by runes to add your own tweaks to rune divination or even invent an entirely new system. In fact, as a beginner, you will be unencumbered by preconceptions and therefore more likely to innovate. Here's an analogy that I like to use when teaching my students: When you learn to sew or knit, you start with a specific set of procedures that work. Then you get creative. As a beginner, one often gets started with a craft by following patterns that are known to work and were made by more advanced practitioners of the art. Creativity comes into play when changing a pattern to fit your own needs or when inventing completely new patterns.

Divining Rune Combinations

You know that runes can be combined to form bindrunes. Up until now, you've been reading runes in divination one at a time. Runes can also be read as bindrunes if they fall near or on top of one another or if pulled from a bag specifically for the purpose of reading as bindrunes. Try pulling two runes at once from your bag of runes and reading them together as if they were a bindrune. Reading the compound meanings of bindrunes while performing divination can increase the spectrum of meanings in a rune reading.

You'll need to draw upon your own intuition when deciding what two runes mean once they're intertwined. One person's reading of a bindrune might not match another's, and indeed this is one reason why runic inscriptions still puzzle archeologists and runeologists today. You'll find that the divinatory meaning of bindrunes shifts according to the topic or focus of the reading as well. For example, fehu and uruz together may mean the strength of uruz helping the success of fehu in a financial reading, or it could mean a stormy home life in a relationship reading.

The following are some more examples of rune combination meanings. You'll note that I haven't included all possible rune combinations and that these meanings might differ from yours. Try writing down some random rune combinations and thinking up personal interpretations.

Thurisaz-Ansuz: When these two runes fall together, it means that something that seems like a misfortune is actually a blessing in disguise. If you've just been rejected by a crush, it means that your crush is not right for you and that somebody better is right around the corner. These runes also ask you to look for the growing opportunities in any problem. If you find yourself yelling at your kids, you might take moments of struggle as opportunities to confront your own flaws and eliminate them.

Raido-Ken: Moss does not cling to a rolling stone, so will you be able to heal only when you move forward. For some reason, you've been hanging onto some old baggage. Problems from your childhood might be preventing you from being successful, and you need to seek help to become more than your past. If you're hanging onto hope that an ex will come back to you, it's time to move on.

Gebo-Wunjo: A surprise gift will give great joy. You might win an award at your work or school for a job well done. More than one person will share your joy, so make sure that you spread the love of this rune combination. If you get an unexpected raise, take your family out to dinner. If a friend gives you a surprise party for your birthday, make sure to return the favor to her on the next holiday.

Hagalaz-Neid: You have to destroy in order to create. It's time to not only say goodbye to something negative in your life but to obliterate it. Throw away old garbage that is cluttering up your garage. Kick an addiction to cigarettes. Get rid of whatever is standing in the way of the lifestyle you need and deserve. There's no way to destroy things cleanly with these two runes. You'll have to kill off obstruction and oppression in your life like you'd kill off weeds.

Isa-Jera: Cut your losses and walk away from the gambling table before you lose everything. You might have spent a lot of money going to school, but if you're failing to enjoy and thrive in your choice of major, it is better to drop out than continue to punish yourself. If you're hoping for a promotion, your boss is just leading you on. Don't raise prices in your business, or you'll see your clients leave.

Eihwaz-Pertho: You're on target to win success, but it will take many more tries before you succeed. The competition is fierce between you and others. If you are applying for jobs, scholarships, or competing for the attentions of a desirable person, you'll need to keep your eye on the long-term prize. Expect delays to success, but success can come.

Algiz-Sowilo: A wonderful friendship is forming. You will meet somebody and it will feel like you have known this person in a previous lifetime. You will find a job or hobby that will fit you like a glove. This rune combination expresses a feeling of comfortable familiarity and trust. When reading on communications, this indicates that a person is telling the truth.

Tiwaz-Berkanan: It is time for some tough love. If you're dealing with friends or family members who are abusing your kindness, it's time to let them see some consequences for their actions. It is possible that you are struggling with yourself and have to treat yourself like a kid for a while. If you've been spending too much on your credit cards, put them in a block of ice in the freezer or cut them up. If you've been avoiding work, turn off the Internet or ground yourself until your homework is finished.

Ehwaz-Mannaz: This combination of runes can represent a soul mate. Loyalty and companionship are represented. With this alliance, you can move farther and faster than you've ever been able to progress before. In business, this represents a powerful merger or a partnership that will take the business to the next level. If you're in a relationship, this rune combination suggests that all that is needed to solve difficulties may be to shift your frame of mind.

Laguz-Ingwaz: The very beginnings of love are happening, and sparks are flying. Emotional love can come from what may seem like just a sexual fling. A friendship can develop into something more. If you're trying to choose between two jobs, choose the one that inspires you rather than the boring one that pays more because this could be the beginning of something greater for you.

Othila-Dagaz: This rune combination represents the cycles of life and death and the pause for breath that happens sometimes in such cycles. A college student may need to move back in with his or her parents for a while after a bad breakup or flunking out of school. A brief fling with an ex might lead to yet another breakup. A sabbatical from a teaching job might lead a tenured faculty member to choose to retire to write romance novels instead of continuing a teaching career.

Creating Personal Divinatory Bindrunes: Making Sigils with Runes to Make New Divination Sets

One frustration that beginning students often have with runes is that their rune readings often seem too vague because of the big concepts embodied by each rune. Some beginners combat the limitations of a small set of runes by adopting additional runic alphabets and rotating or combining sets of runes. You can also develop your own bindrunes to add to your runes that have significant meanings for you. There's no rune that precisely tells you that your car will break down, so go ahead and make one. There's not yet a rune for when your work computer goes on the fritz, but you can easily add one to your runes. The runes you select to combine to make the meanings you need may be different from the ones that I've shared in this book, and that's okay. You're trying to evoke meanings from your own brain, and everyone operates a little bit differently. You might even find yourself adding embellishments and symbols that don't come from any known runic system.

Here's one way that I like to brainstorm new bindrunes that I need: I turn back to my rune journal and look at the daily runes that I have pulled and the life events that happened as a result. I once suddenly found myself struggling with being chronically late for appointments. I absolutely abhor being late for anything. When I had a twenty-mile commute to work as a schoolteacher, I would leave two hours early and sometimes sit in the parking lot waiting for the custodian to unlock the school doors, so terrified was I of tardiness. I even find myself leaving early to get to events at which my lateness wouldn't be noticed, such as library story time for the kids. My husband is endlessly annoyed by the fact that we're always the first family to show up to every party we attend because I shoot for the start time.

I'd rather be two hours early than two minutes late for anything, so imagine my consternation when I had a series of events in my life that led to being late to doctor appointments, school drop-offs for the kids, and other random outings. Each individual event of lateness seemed to be random—the result of unpreventable circumstances. So I turned to the runes for a little help. At first, I looked through my rune journal to see if the daily rune draw happened to be the same rune each time I was late. Nope. That would be too easy. However, I did notice a pattern of some runes showing up more than others on days when I ran late or came close to running late. Laguz and dagaz seemed to make themselves known in my daily readings around this time, which I interpreted as a message to relax my emotions and get a jump-start on each day. My original interpretations remained true, and indeed staying calm and leaving early are two things that I do to combat late arrivals. However, to get more of a head's up about when I might run into another lateness situation, I created a new rune that was a bindrune of laguz and dagaz and added it to the sack of runes from which I did my daily draw. If I pulled my new "lateness" rune, I would make certain to leave much earlier and to let people know I might run late that day.

If I had designed a lateness bindrune by thinking about all the runes and putting two together that make sense, I might have chosen an entirely different rune combination such as raido and isa, which might have worked just as well. However, by retroactively gaining meaning from how the runes expressed themselves in my life in the past, I feel that I got to know those runes a little more. From re-examining them, I was able to see a new side to some old friends and otherwise expand my knowledge and interpretation of the runes. I highly recommend that beginners record and review how their runic divination turns out to build upon their own understanding of the runes, resulting in divination that is more practical and potentially more accurate.

Runic Wheels

There is a special kind of bindrune called a runic wheel that is popular because of its beauty and usefulness for meditation, given that it looks like a mandala, and it feels like you're making a mandala if you draw a particularly complex runic wheel. The central rune on a runic wheel is the subject or start of your knowing. For example, if your runic wheel was going to protect or enhance your mind or a person, you might have mannaz in the very center of your wheel. One should always carve the center rune or runes first and add more later, starting with a ring around the center stave or staves and, if necessary, adding outer rings around that. Around the outer edges of the runic wheel are modifiers, or those poetic phrases and adjectives that you might add to your knowing.

To "Fix" Runic Inscriptions You or Others Have Made

I was asked when writing this book what thing I would do differently if I went back to being a beginner with the runes. I definitely did not keep enough records of my learning when I was just starting out, though I did try somewhat. I had a rune journal, dream journal, and scrapbook in which I wrote down the spiritual exercises that worked for me. However, I only added the rune inscriptions for spiritual exercises in which I had tried and proven their efficacy. There were many magic spells, chants, and meditations that I attempted, saw no positive results for, and immediately gave up on. I'd burn up any runic objects made during the failed spiritual exercise and allow myself to forget about my failures. I run into this same pattern in other areas of my life as well. I've been learning to dance for a few years and, now that I have intermediate level skills, I wish that I had made more videos of myself as a beginner so that I can see my accomplishments more clearly.

The added bonus of keeping records of all of your spiritual exercises that involve runes is that, even if they don't work, you may be able to make minor revisions later when you have more experience and see them work very well. I've worked throughout this book to show you that you have a lot of freedom and leeway when it comes to the runes, but that doesn't mean that there's no right way or wrong way to do things. The tricky thing about real magic work is that there actually is a right way for you to create results in your life. It may take much experimentation and many changes to be able to make your runes work best for you.

In general, runemasters agree that poorly designed runic inscriptions can be "fixed" to work more effectively. You will necessarily have to carve the runes all over again, since it's ineffective to cross out any misspelled words: that alone does not destroy the energy and will mar your inscription with distractions to your focus. You'll have to repair the energy of your runes as well by charging them anew. Most runemasters try to prevent bad runic inscriptions in the first place or by reviewing some of the rules already learned and checking to see if spaces can be removed or if the inscription can be condensed and made more efficient on a rough draft on a piece of paper. As you gain more experience, you may be able to see how some runes work better for your purposes than the ones you chose in the past for a specific spiritual exercise. Don't shy away from failure as you learn. Remember your mistakes and carefully build upon your previous knowledge.

Hiding Runes in Plain Sight for Divination and for Empowerment

Runes are forever around us; we just have to look in order to see them. There's an urban legend I'm often asked about that suggests runes are hidden in bar codes on packaging. Since bar codes are just bars, unless you're talking about isa, no runes can be easily discerned in plain sight in the average barcode. However, runes make their appearances in many corporate logos, in other branding marks, or in cultural iconography. One can observe that the peace sign has algiz, the rune of friendship and protection from the Elder Futhark, upside down and enclosed in a circle. Some believe that the peace sign actually depicts a rune from the Younger Futhark that means death since it looks like algiz flipped upside down, but that meaning seems to be less of a fit to me.

I've also noticed that the Bluetooth symbol is a bindrune of hagalaz (of the Younger Futhark) and berkanan. Recall that, in ancient times, runes could be written from left to right or right to left, or even one line in one direction and the next line in an opposite direction. Staves were often written backward or even upside-down with no known reason. When interpreting runes that you find out in the world, keep in mind that the runes can be facing in any direction or combined with any other rune.

You can hide runes in order to discreetly use them for spiritual empowerment or to have a secret set of runes just for fun. Runes themselves are a secret code for the powers of life. In this era of information, when the meanings of the runes can be looked up instantly on the Internet, a beginner may be puzzled by the fact that I allude to the keeping of sacred secrets, so I'd like to speak to the value of secrecy.

First, the runes have to be experienced in order to be learned, lived, and believed. I don't think that one beginner is going to look through this book, close the cover, and believe that the runes have every power I say they do. A student who practices real experiential learning will be the student who truly understands that runes work. I could write runes as big as the Hollywood sign and the general public wouldn't know all of the runic mysteries. As much as it pains me to say it as an author and a reader, books aren't enough to solve sacred mysteries. Runes are like music in that they can cause emotion and express concepts that mere words cannot touch.

Second, it is okay to keep sacred things private. You don't owe a translation of your hidden runes to anyone but yourself; it's between you and the divine. Privacy can be a rare thing for me. I'm a public figure, and at home I have young kids, so privacy is often a joke. With the runes, I can respectfully keep some information private. My family knows that when I'm in my sacred temple room working on something, I am not to be disturbed and no questions are to be asked about my specific activities. Much of my personal religious practice is private because it's simply too personal to share and is my business alone. You don't have to keep your runes secret, but if you do, have confidence that you deserve to do so and don't let anyone bully you into revealing your personal business.

Secrecy also keeps things special. If everyone used the runes as an everyday script, they would no longer be special. People wouldn't have to undertake serious study to learn how to use the runes, and thus they might seem boring and too mundane. If you use the runes to write your grocery-shopping list, it might be difficult to turn around and try to use them to evoke the sacred powers of the divine. As a beginner, it is fine to give yourself lots of practice with the runes. But as you gain confidence with your knowledge of them, consider reserving their use for special occasions if you find they begin to lose their novelty. Personally, even though I use them frequently, the thrill of the runes never fades. And my love of runes is still going strong despite having to work so intensely with them as an author of a rune book.

Another reason to keep secrets is to avoid spoiling surprises. When I teach students about the runes, I don't automatically translate every bindrune I show them, but ask curious questions about what each student thinks the bindrune means to him or her. We all know that the experience of a surprise party or a gift without occasion can brighten one's mood more than an anticipated event. Mystery and wonderment can add to any experience. When I handed over a "lucky magic charm" to my father before his surgery, I didn't explain to him the minutia of how I made the charm or what each individual rune meant. Knowing that there were secret formulas involved in what I was doing was enough to enhance my dad's belief that my lucky charm could work. Don't guilt trip yourself into thinking you're being deceptive if you don't have a full public debriefing of every rune that you use around friends and loved ones, even if you are using the runes on those friends and loved ones. It's enough to get permission to "pray" or make a magic charm for someone and then allow the enigmatic details to surprise and delight.

Your kids don't need to know how electrical systems work in order to flip on a light switch for them, and likewise you don't have to explain how the runes are at work on their school textbook covers to help them pay attention as they read, unless you want to.

Finally, there is something sacred about the act of keeping secrets. I learned from several of my spiritual teachers that the four powers of the magician are to know, to dare, to will, and to keep silent. It's easy to see how boldness, force of will, and knowledge are all powerful things, but silence is just as powerful. Gurus, monks, and priests of some religions take vows of silence for long periods of time. Silence allows the ability to listen. And keeping private things sacred instead of blabbing about them in public or on social media can be a welcome respite from oversharing. As a talkative Gemini, I know that silence can be like a muscle that needs to be developed over time and flexed on occasion. I used to blab just about every thought that tiptoed its way across my mind, mistaking verbosity for honesty. As I developed my own spirituality, I found that keeping quiet about what I was doing helped me to focus on my work and devote myself to the task of the present moment. When I retreat to my temple room to work with runes, I am not simultaneously thinking up ways to describe my accomplishments later to my followers on social media or to my family; I'm just doing my work.

For all these reasons and more, you may wish to encrypt your runes or make them even more secretive than they already are, but you don't have to if you don't want to. Of course you can also develop your own methods of secreting away your runes. If you do design a secret code, remember to write down a key to your encryption. You can hide the key somewhere, like a locked trunk or a file with a password on your computer, but don't skip the vital step of writing down how you made the code. I wrote some rune codes years ago and, in some cases, I can't make heads or tails of my encrypted runes now even though I was sure at the time that I'd remember my new "ingenious" system.

The following are two simple ways to encrypt your runes for the sake of secrecy.

Numbers

Since each rune has a number, you can simply write down a number in place of a rune when you want to be discreet about that rune. Instead of writing the stave for fehu on your laptop for success, you can write the number one and charge it with fehu, for example. Using numbers has limitations if you're working with more than one rune, however, because adding numbers together or writing them too close together might obscure their meanings so much that even you become confused.

Tree Runes

Try using tree runes, which are a common rune encryption system that involves numbers. Remember that the Elder Futhark runes are written in three aettir of eight. Tree runes look a little bit like trees: the branches represent the rune's number. Branches that lead off to the left represent the rune aett, and branches off to the right represent the number of the rune within that aett. Fehu would have one branch to the left and one branch to the right because it is in the first aett and is the first rune within that particular aett.

Rune Tree Example for Fehu

Rune trees are a more artful way to disguise runes that you want to place on talismans or other public objects. It is also possible to write with rune trees as a script. Decoding rune trees is a project that will take you some time if you forget what you wrote later on. Since rune trees are so artful and repetitive, they make fine decorative borders for things and rune wheels made from rune trees can be positively mesmerizing to look at. Experiment with rune trees to see what beautiful art you can create.

In the example below, I've disguised the rune wheel To Break a Curse, taught in chapter 5, by using rune trees. If you know your enemy is a skilled magician, he or she might try to use your runes against you. A person can more easily hex you if he or she knows your true name or intentions, which are spelled out in your runes. By hiding ken, thurisaz, and, uruz with rune trees, you protect your own strong magic so that your spell can't be broken. It is still possible for a malevolent person who is well-versed in runes to decipher your rune tree if you leave it lying around for him or her to study at length, but a rune tree will protect from casual observation and also tricks the eye of one very familiar with runes into not recognizing it as a rune right away. A rune tree swinging from a pendant or nestled amongst other trees in a painting can be easily overlooked. Your enemy would likely have to be looking for a rune tree, so don't go bragging about your amazing skills in this area.

Below is an unbreakable anticurse helm of awe that uses rune trees.

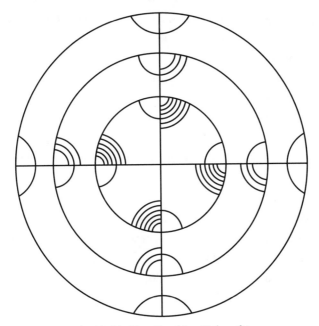

Unbreakable Hex-Breaking Helm of Awe

Designing a Personalized Runic System

Imagine having your own secret fortune-telling stones that represent a map to your own personal inner consciousness. You can become an expert in your very own system for telling the future and revealing the secrets of the past. Your specialized magical tools and knowledge can be passed down to your children, can be shared like a secret language between you and your lover, or can be kept as a sacred treasure for only you to know. Learning divination by creating your own system of runes is kind of like decoding your own genetic code or being able to explore the deepest regions of your own subconscious. I've included creative exercises in this book not because they're easy but because they give beginners the best foundation in the concepts to help them realize that runes are just tools to release the power and knowledge stored within each person.

I've made many sets of my own rune systems in my lifetime. Of course, the runes I invented as a child don't look like the runes I designed as an adult, and that's okay. Change and evolution are natural as you grow spiritually throughout your life. It's easy to get overwhelmed as a beginner and think that you need to include everything in your divinatory rune system, but bigger is not necessarily better. Consider the four alchemical elements of earth, air, water, and fire; the four elements together symbolically represent the totality of matter in the universe and there are only four of them. A bigger alphabet wouldn't necessarily allow me to write a book with more thoughts or speak language more clearly.

A good place to start is to think about what number of runes you'd like in your system. The Witch's Runes have thirteen, but you can have even less to make things simpler. I suspect that thirteen runes were selected in the modern divination system as a nod to the magical nature of the number thirteen. Here are some other number associations that I, and some numerologists, make:

Two: A set of two runes, such as creating one that means "yes" and one that means "no," represents the duality or polarity of the divine between light and dark, good and evil, feminine and masculine, yin and yang, or other matched pairs.

Three: Add the independence of the number one to the loving pair of the number two and you get three. I always think of the number three as the divine child of the Goddess and the God of my religion represented by the number two. When one and two combine to make three, the three are now the Goddess, God, and divine child. It is a number, then, of growth and completion. The triangle is a very stable shape, too, so a simple rune set of three can be complete.

Four: If you made runes for the four elements, they would form four stable and complete quarters. Any set of runes with four is stable. I always think of the number four as the four legs of a table that keep it operating as a solid and trustworthy foundation for work. If you need runes to read on topics of creating a foundation in your life, consider making them a set of four.

Five: A set of five runes would be a good one for teasing apart the chaos of interpersonal relationships like friendships or alliances and squabbles with coworkers. The number five is an unstable one, so it is associated with the constant destruction and creation required for growth.

Six: The number six is another stable even number, often associated with both literal and figurative journeys. If you'd like to make a set of runes for your school career, for example, I'd advise it to be made up of six runes. If you want to make a special traveling set of runes, used to read on your trips, on the ups and downs of travel itself, I'd suggest making six runes. Airport security has carefully examined my runes before but has always let them through without quibbling.

Seven: Seven has always been my favorite number, and it is the number of magic and mystery. Make rune sets dedicated to spiritual exploration out of runes that number seven. It's an odd number, so there's a bit of that unpredictable instability in the energy of seven, but such is life. Think of the odd number above the serene growth of the number six as the wild card that the universe throws into your life to create change.

Eight: As we climb higher, the numbers represent greater degrees of completion and success. The number eight represents taking achievements that already exist in your life to the next level. If you want to make a rune set just for your career path, consider creating that set of runes with eight sigils.

Nine: In Chinese numerology, the number nine is very lucky, and this meaning carries over to Western numerology since it is a high number representing completion. Make nine runes that each symbolize the joys in your life. You can pull out your special set of runes when you're feeling depressed and they can help you navigate through the blues.

The above numbers can be added together to make larger sets of runes with a number of runes that has a significant meaning, but remember that simplicity can be best. Here's a brainstorming trick I use when I'm designing a new rune set: I make a pie chart with the number of sections equal to the number of runes I'll be using. Try this for yourself. Get a large piece of paper and draw a big circle. Draw lines to divide the circle into the number of runes you've chosen. The pie chart you are creating is a visual reminder that all your runes together represent the totality of the universe or the realm that you want your runes to describe. So if you are making a set of career runes, the runes together represent all possible career potentials for you.

From here on out, your rune creation is limited only by your imagination. You can divide your diagram in half and make half the runes negative and half the runes positive, or you can keep everything upbeat if you like. You can start making bindrunes based on the notes in your journal or begin drawing symbols that bubble up from your own mind unhindered by anyone else's drawings. By the time you're finished, you'll have learned a lot about yourself, and you'll be ready to learn even more by using them for divination. Remember to write down your rune meanings in your rune journal. You are the leading expert in the world on your own personal set of runes, so don't let the knowledge you gain be lost to the ages.

conclusion

Some runeologists call runes both an art and a science because the world is at the leading edge of rune research right now. We can all add to the corpus of rune knowledge as it evolves. No matter if it's your first or fifth divinatory tool, I hope that you are able to connect to the earth and use runes.

Dive into rune studies with enthusiasm as a beginner. Make a set of runes and then make another one that is even better than the first. Read every book that you can get your hands on about runes, even the ones that have ideas with which you might disagree. Reach out to try to find runemasters and runeologists in your area. In the Seattle area, we're blessed with a Nordic Heritage Museum that can be visited to learn more about the culture and history of ancient people who used runes. If you're lucky, you might even find workshops about runes being taught at metaphysical bookstores or other venues near you. Find local fortune-tellers and ask if you can buy a rune reading. I often learn so much more about being a better fortune-teller by watching how others perform readings.

Most of all, please keep practicing with your runes in order to keep their meanings fresh in your mind and their use as a divinatory tool relevant in your life. Perhaps you will be the next person to develop an innovative runecast or system of runes. You're already the world's leading expert on your own mind, and you have special gifts to share with the world. Through the language of the runes, we can all read the stories about the inner landscapes of our minds and discover what the divine has yet to write in the chapters of our lives. I pray that the ending of this book marks just the beginning of your story with the runes.

glossary

Aett: The Elder Futhark runes are organized into three families of eight called aettir. The first aett is ruled by fertility gods; the second, starting with hagalaz, by protection deities; and the third, starting with tiwaz, by deities of divine justice and order.

Aspect: A rune's relationship with another rune in a spread or runecast. In general, runes that are across from one another on a diagram are negatively affecting one another. Runes at a 90-degree angle from one another on a circular diagram indicate that they may block or oppose one another. Runes at a 45-degree angle or less from one another positively affect or support one another.

Bindrune: Two or more runes combined to form a compound meaning.

Kenning: See knowing.

Knowing: A poetic, descriptive name for something, often extolling virtues or describing its true purpose.

Magic: The art of creating change within yourself or your world to match your true will. Real magic can be performed with runes.

Runecast: Runes cast onto a surface or chart or laid out individually in specific patterns that give context to their meanings.

Runa: Runemaster. A wise or cunning man or woman.

Runemaster: One who works with runes. See runemistress.

Runemistress: A modern feminine form of runemaster.

Runeologist: One who is devoted to the study and interpretation of rune staves as an ancient script.

Runestaff: A wand or walking stick carved with runes for spiritual purposes.

Runwita: Runemaster. A wise or cunning man or woman.

Script: A letter system used for writing words.

Sigil: A symbol that has a powerful meaning and is often used as a talisman.

Stave: A written rune; a runic letter.

World tree: A symbolic framework for the universe from ancient Norse mythology as well as other mythologies and religions.

recommended reading

Fitch, Ed. *The Rites of Odin*. St. Paul, MN: Llewellyn Publications, 1990.

Hulse, David Allen. *The Western Mysteries: An Encyclopedic Guide to the Sacred Languages & Magickal Systems of the World; The Key of It All, Book II*. St. Paul, MN: Llewellyn Publications, 2000.

Olsen, Kaedrich. *Runes for Transformation: Using Ancient Symbols to Change Your Life*. San Francisco: Weiser Books, 2008.

Pennick, Nigel. *The Complete Illustrated Guide to Runes: How to Interpret the Ancient Wisdom of the Runes.* Boston: Element Books Inc., 1999.

Sheppard, Susan. *A Witch's Runes: How to Make and Use Your Own Magick Stones.* Secaucus, NJ: Citadel Press, 1998.

bibliography

Aswynn, Freya. *Northern Mysteries & Magick: Runes & Feminine Powers.* St. Paul, MN: Llewellyn Publications, 1998.

Blake, Deborah. *Witchcraft on a Shoestring: Practicing the Craft Without Breaking Your Budget.* Woodbury, MN: Llewellyn Publications, 2010.

Conway, D.J. *Norse Magic.* Woodbury, MN: Llewellyn Publications, 1990.

Cunningham, Scott. *Divination for Beginners: Reading the Past, Present & Future.* St. Paul, MN: Llewellyn Publications, 2003.

Grimassi, Raven. *Hereditary Witchcraft: Secrets of the Old Religion.* Woodbury, MN: Llewellyn Publications, 1999.

Harl, Kenneth W. *The Vikings.* Chantilly, VA: The Teaching Company, 2005.

Luna, Bianca. *Runes Guidebook.* Torino, Italy: Lo Scarabeo, 2011.

Melville, Francis. *The Book of Runes: Read the Secrets in the Language of the Stones.* London: Quarto Publishing, 2003.

Page, R. I. *Runes: Reading the Past.* Berkeley, CA: University of California Press, 1987.

Peschel, Lisa. *A Practical Guide to the Runes: Their Uses in Divination and Magick.* St. Paul, MN: Llewellyn Publications, 1989.

Saint-Germain, Jon. *Runic Palmistry.* St. Paul, MN: Llewellyn Publications, 2001.

Thorsson, Edred. *Northern Magic: Rune Mysteries and Shamanism.* St. Paul, MN: Llewellyn Publications, 1992.

Tyson, Donald. *Runic Astrology: Chart Interpretation Through the Runes.* Woodbury, MN: Llewellyn Publications, 2009.

Acknowledgments

I am grateful for the hard work on this book done by editors, including Amy Glaser and Lauryn Heineman. Without the brilliant minds in Llewellyn's editing, marketing, publicity, and art departments, this book would not be able to appropriately add to the body of lore surrounding runes.

To Write to the Author

If you wish to contact the author or would like more information about this book, please write to the author in care of Llewellyn Worldwide Ltd. and we will forward your request. Both the author and publisher appreciate hearing from you and learning of your enjoyment of this book and how it has helped you. Llewellyn Worldwide Ltd. cannot guarantee that every letter written to the author can be answered, but all will be forwarded. Please write to:

Alexandra Chauran
⁒ Llewellyn Worldwide
2143 Wooddale Drive
Woodbury, MN 55125-2989

Please enclose a self-addressed stamped envelope for reply,
or $1.00 to cover costs. If outside the U.S.A., enclose
an international postal reply coupon.

Many of Llewellyn's authors have websites with additional information and resources. For more information, please visit our website at http://www.llewellyn.com.